Efronia

Women's Life Writings from Around the World

Edited by Marilyn Yalom

EFRONIA

*An
Armenian
Love
Story*

Stina Katchadourian

*Based on a memoir
by Efronia Katchadourian*

Translated by Herant Katchadourian

Northeastern University Press Boston

To the memory of Efronia Katchadourian

Northeastern University Press

Copyright 1993 by Stina Katchadourian

Library of Congress Cataloging-in-Publication Data
Katchadourian, Stina.
    Efronia : an Armenian love story / Stina Katchadourian.
        p.   cm.—(Women's life writings from around the world)
    Based on an unpublished memoir by Efronia Katchadourian
translated by Herant Katchadourian.
    Includes bibliographical references.
    ISBN 1-55553-172-5—ISBN 1-55553-180-6 (pbk.)
    1. Katchadourian, Efronia, 1894–1986. 2. Women—Armenia—
Biography. 3. Armenian massacres, 1915–1923. I. Katchadourian,
Efronia, 1894–1986. II. Title. III. Series.
CT 1919.A758K384   1993
956.6'202'092—dc20   93-2477
[B]

Designed by Milenda Nan Ok Lee

Composed in Garamond #3 by Coghill Composition Co., Richmond, Virginia. Printed and bound by The Maple Press, York, Pennsylvania. The paper is Sebago Antique, an acid-free sheet.

MANUFACTURED IN THE UNITED STATES OF AMERICA
98 97 96 95 94 93   5 4 3 2 1

Contents

Contents

Illustrations

Foreword

Efronia is the first book in a series of women's memoirs in translation published by Northeastern University Press. This series springs from three related sources: an ongoing interest in women's lives, a growing body of scholarship on self-referential literature, and the need to extend the knowledge of women's life-writing beyond linguistic barriers.

Once the stepsister of both literature and history, autobiography was considered too close to reality to be the former and too fanciful to be the latter. Today, literary works called "memoirs," "autobiographies," or "personal narratives" are widely appreciated for a variety of reasons, including their psychological revelations and their documentary value. In our largely impersonal, often overgrown, and frequently uncontrollable world, the first-person story offers reassurance to countless readers eager to discover how someone else has found a way through the hazards of life.

Unfortunately, the number of English translations of personal narratives has lagged behind the demand for them, and especially those authored by women. Even many major European autobiographies are largely unknown beyond their national boundaries. The recent group translation of George Sand's monumental *History of My Life* is but one example, albeit an important one, of works that should have long been available to an English readership. Moreover, we should not make the mistake of considering autobiography an exclusively Western phenomenon resulting from our post-Renaissance history of individualism. Long before the groundswell of autobiographies inaugurated, in the late eighteenth century, by the publication of Rousseau's *Confessions*, there were scattered cases of "I" stories in Asian languages such as Japanese, as well as in most European languages. In our own time, narratives of the self proliferate among writers not only in Europe and the Americas but in every country of the world.

Efronia belongs to a rare autobiographical variety in that the memoirs upon which it is based were written by an Armenian woman in her late eighties. She recorded her history for her son, who translated it into English when his mother was on her deathbed. A few years after Efronia's death, her daughter-in-law, Stina, framed Efronia's life within her historical times, both in the Middle East, where she lived for the greater part of the century, and in California, where she was transplanted when she was eighty-two. The relationship between these two women, one whose native languages were Armenian and Turkish and the other whose native languages were Swedish and Finnish, gives this work a cross-cultural complexity that is especially appropriate for the inauguration of a translation series.

Efronia corresponds in every way to the selection criteria we originally set forth for this series. First, it extends our knowledge of the female experience in a specific time and place—in this case, in early twentieth-century Ottoman Turkey. Second, *Efronia* is a literary work in the broadest sense—that is, it interests and moves and enlightens us by virtue of its meaningful content and aesthetic integrity. Third, the eloquent persona of its main narrator makes us care about her destiny.

We encounter in *Efronia* two clear voices, that of the protagonist, Efronia Katchadourian, and that of the second narrator, Stina Katchadourian. In this respect, *Efronia* is a quintessentially "female" piece of literature, for the tradition of women writing the biographies of their mothers (or mothers-in-law) with their own stories squeezed into the interstices extends back at least two hundred years. More currently, in the late twentieth century, women authors have interwoven the stories of mothers, grandmothers, aunts, sisters, daughters, female friends, and even mythical women into works that shift back and forth from biography to autobiography with a specifically feminine ease—for example, Kim Chernin's *In My Mother's House*, Maxine Hong Kingston's *The Woman Warrior*, and Sissela Bok's biography of her mother, Alva Myrdal.

Efronia Katchadourian's memories of love and survival in Ottoman Turkey make an unforgettable tale—unforgettable for the protagonist three score years after the world war that racked her life, unforgettable for the reader, who now has the opportunity of entering Efronia's tumultuous world.

MARILYN YALOM
Institute for Research on Women and Gender
Stanford University

Introduction

My mother-in-law, Efronia Katchadourian (1894–1986), is buried in a secluded creekside cemetery in northern California. Her grave, shaded by live oaks and redwoods, faces the high school both her grandchildren attended. It is also close to the university campus where her only son teaches. Had someone told the young Efronia, growing up in the Ottoman Empire, that this would be her final resting place, she might not have found it surprising. Although her hometown of Aintab (Gaziantep) on the Anatolian high plateau in Turkey seems many worlds away from the American West Coast, it had always had its share of enterprising young Armenian men hoping to make their fortune in the New World. With the hard work and good business sense characteristic of their people, they often succeeded, and many returned to their native communities to choose a bride. The attractive young Efronia herself received many inquiries from suitors who wanted nothing more than to offer her the good life in their new country. But for years, to her family's puzzlement and frustration, she turned them all down. In this book, written very near the end of her life, she explains why.

If burial in California might not have been so difficult for the young Efronia to imagine, having a daughter-in-law like me certainly would have been. Had her life followed a predictable course, she would have attended a college run by American Protestant missionaries not far away from the town where she grew up. She might have become a teacher and taught for a few years before getting married and having children. Later, she would have had considerable say in choosing her son's Armenian bride.

None of this happened. During the fall Efronia planned to enter Marash College for Girls, the First World War broke out. Instead of being a student, she became a witness to what we today would call an ethnic cleansing, directed at her people: the first genocide of modern times. Although her family survived, her world was changed forever.

If Efronia would have found it hard to believe she would end up with a European daughter-in-law, the reverse is also true. The First World War had shattered Efronia's youth; the Second World War cast its shadow over mine. Few people left the war-torn Finland where I grew up. Long-distance travel meant taking the overnight steamer to neutral Sweden, where people were well dressed, where you could buy candy and other sweets, and where there were no bombed-out ruins. Even though Finland had become less isolated by the time I entered college, it still seemed a foregone conclusion that I would settle there. Most likely, one of the women who had scraped and struggled to feed her family during the war years and whose husband had been fighting at the Russian front would be my future mother-in-law.

With luck, this mother-in-law would have been a benevolently distant presence in my life, sparing with her advice and aware of my need to regard us both as independent women on an equal footing. I would certainly not have expected her to call me "my daughter," with all this implied of supervision on her part and submissiveness on mine. Years later, though, that is precisely what Efronia did, effusively and enthusiastically. I wanted to duck for cover, until the day I realized the strength of our bond, as she saw it.

The occasion was the first large family gathering at our new home in a mountain village above Beirut. Uncharacteristically, my mother-in-law did not volunteer to cook. I had the distinct and uncomfortable feeling that the gathering was meant to showcase my culinary talents for the large extended family. I decided to make—without the benefit of a recipe—the only Scandinavian dish I knew how to prepare, Swedish meatballs.

When we began to eat, a silence fell over the room. As mouths puckered and one relative after another reached for more water, I realized that something was drastically wrong. I tasted a meatball: it was as salty as the Dead Sea.

It was then that my mother-in-law spoke up. Fixing everyone in the room with her matriarchal gaze, she declared: "You can never trust these local butchers. They have pre-salted the meat again."

That moment, for me, defines unconditional love. I realized that from now on, in the eyes of this mother-in-law, her daughter-in-law could do no wrong. And year after year, the manifestations of her love continued—in the form of presents, practical help, food, birthday cards, and, most importantly, an ever-vigilant presence that proclaimed, with the primordial strength of a guardian angel, "I'm here whenever you need me."

I often wondered where this strength came from. By any ordinary standard, Efronia had endured enough hardship in her life to make her an embittered and constricted person. How could she be so expansive, joyous, and forward-looking? It seemed a mystery to me.

I have tried, in this book, to provide sufficient context and background so that my mother-in-law can answer that question herself. She will not do it directly, because the question was never put to her directly, and she was not very introspective. But the answer is there, nevertheless. Embedded in her story about personal love and loss is also the story of the regenerative powers of the human spirit.

That, I think, is the deepest reason why she wanted so much to have this story told.

Stanford, California   STINA KATCHADOURIAN
January 1993

Acknowledgments

My mother-in-law, Efronia, had very little time to follow the birth process of this book before she passed away. However, she left no doubt that she was very keen on having her story told and that she thoroughly approved of what I was trying to do. For her encouragement, for the effort it took to write her story down, and for the courage it took to remember, she has my deep gratitude.

This book could not have come into being without the help of my husband, Herant. Not only did he translate his mother's manuscript—a process that brought mother and son closer than they had ever been before—but from the outset he also supported my idea of telling the story from an "outsider's" perspective. His perceptive criticism, his support, and his practical help throughout this project have been of crucial importance to me.

For careful readings, encouragement, and support, my sincere thanks go to Bengt Ahlfors, Beverly Allen, Mary Catherine Bateson, Susan Groag Bell, Poppy Stenius Berghem, Vida Bertrand, Sissela Bok, Birgitta Boucht, Alev Lytle Croutier, Ann DeBusk, the late Arturo Islas, my daughter, Nina Katchadourian, my sister, Maj Kuhlefelt, Merete Mazzarella, Mary Jane Moffatt, Nancy Packer, Janet James Purdy, Märta Tikkanen, Tania Tour-Sarkissian, Patricia Willrich, Esther Wojcicki, Susan Wojcicki, and Irvin Yalom. I am

grateful to Margo Davis for the use of her photograph of
Efronia. My thanks also to Professor Richard Hovannissian of
UCLA and Professor Robert Melson of Purdue University,
whose helpful suggestions on the historical aspects of this
story are much appreciated. I, of course, take the entire
responsibility for any remaining inaccuracies.

I also want to express my appreciation and thanks to my
Armenian relatives. My mother-in-law occupied a central place
in their lives. Their support of this project has been very
important to me.

Marilyn Yalom, editor of this series, deserves a very special
thanks. A demanding critic as well as a true believer in this
book throughout its birth process, she is really its midwife.

Part I

EFRONIA

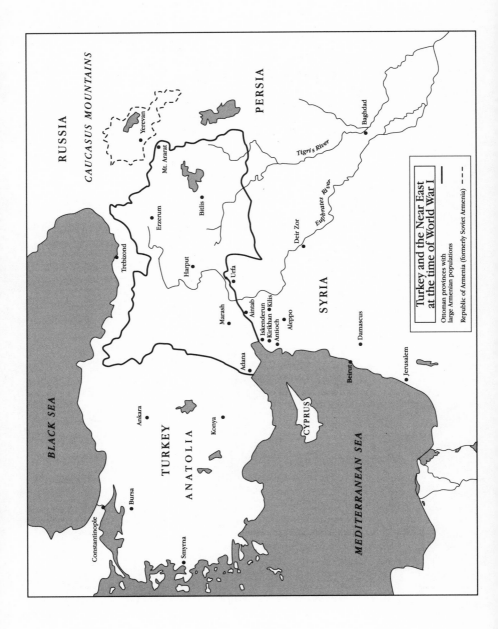

RUSSIA

CAUCASUS MOUNTAINS

PERSIA

Yerevan

Mt. Ararat

Baghdad

Tigris River

Erzerum

Bitlis

Euphrates River

Deir Zor

Trebizond

Harput

Urfa

SYRIA

Marash

Aintab

Iskenderun · Kilis

Kirikhan · Aleppo

Antioch

Damascus

Adana

Jerusalem

Beirut

BLACK SEA

Ankara

Konya

TURKEY

ANATOLIA

CYPRUS

Bursa

MEDITERRANEAN SEA

Constantinople

Smyrna

Turkey and the Near East
at the time of World War I

Ottoman provinces with
large Armenian populations

Republic of Armenia (formerly Soviet Armenia)

I

A Secret Almost Buried

"Always remember: in every situation in life, you have to use your head," my mother-in-law, Efronia, often used to say, and to everyone who knew her, she seemed to have followed that principle to the letter.

Life had presented Efronia with ample opportunities for losing her head, right up to the moment during the civil war in Beirut when she heard a loud knock on her front door. She opened it to three hot-headed guerrilla fighters, hand grenades hanging from their belts like huge grapes, who were pointing their rifles at her.

"Someone is sniping at our position from your apartment. We demand to come in and search."

Efronia smiled. "Why, of course, dear boys. By all means. Come right in. But I'll tell you, the only people here are myself and Lucine, here, who is my helper."

The guerrillas blustered in and searched every corner of the apartment, which was near the Jardin Publique.

Meanwhile, Lucine went to the kitchen and prepared five cups of Turkish coffee.

"My boys, you must be tired from all that fighting," said Efronia. "Come, sit down here and have some coffee. Lucine made a little *paklava* yesterday. It's delicious. Please help yourselves."

The guerrillas, looking slightly humiliated, asked: "Madame, you are not afraid of us?"

Efronia smiled at them and looked heavenward. "My dear boys, God is in heaven, and you are here. How could I possibly be afraid?"

Two weeks later, with the fighting raging in her neighborhood, her "dear boys" helped Efronia, Lucine, and their two suitcases into an armored vehicle that took them to the airport and a flight to Paris.

From there, she called her son in northern California to say she was on her way.

Efronia arrived in San Francisco shortly after her eighty-second birthday.

The civil war in Lebanon had scattered to the four winds a large extended family of which Efronia was the undisputed head. In California, she proceeded to keep this family together in spirit by acting as if nothing had been lost.

She began every new day in the small apartment on Williams Street in Palo Alto that she shared with her companion, Lucine, as if she were expecting scores of visitors. Immaculately dressed, her Clairol Deep Brunette hair neatly swept back into a bun, she positioned herself with her knitting on the sofa overlooking their little back garden. Ramrod straight, partly because of the corset she always wore, she issued the marching orders for the day to Lucine: what to get from the grocery store, when to do the washing, what to have for lunch.

Efronia and Lucine adapted to their new life in California with great resourcefulness. They established routines: Tuesday was shopping day, Thursday laundry day, Friday housecleaning and bath day. They got to know their neighbors, who soon became addicted to Turkish coffee and sesame cookies. They bought an old sewing machine and made slipcovers for the sofa and chairs. Houseplants started thriving on the bookshelf, and geraniums and fuchsias lured hummingbirds to their back porch. They put food by in the old way, and their larder was always full of home-cured olives and home-canned peaches and homemade pickles. Red peppers to be made into paste would be drying on the porch, and they would buy onions by the fifty-pound bag "for the winter."

Still, they had a lot of time on their hands. That is how the idea of the memoir came to me.

"*Aghchigs*," Efronia used to say, "my daughter, a lot of people live such quiet lives. They are born, they live in one place, and then they die. In my life, there has been enough happening to fill up many books."

I had been praying for this opportunity.

"*Medzmama*," I asked, "Grandmother, how would you like to write down the story of your life?"

It was as if she had been waiting to be asked. "I'll begin tomorrow. But I'll need lots of paper."

The next day I went out and bought a package of two hundred sheets of college-ruled paper and a binder.

"There is much to tell," she said. "You may have to get me some more paper later."

Efronia never talked about her writing. She would just disappear once in a while to sit at her bedroom desk and write. Now and then, she would ask for more paper.

A couple of years later, Efronia told her son, Herant: "My dear, I'm finished with the writing. You may read it now."

Then she added, with a little smile, "There will be some things that are new to you."

Efronia handed him the manuscript. There were five hundred pages of neat Armenian handwriting.

Two weeks later, as I was getting ready for bed, Herant

took his mother's manuscript to our living room. "I'll catch up with you soon," he said. "I'll just read a few pages of this. She keeps asking if I've read it yet."

At two o'clock in the morning, I woke up with a start. Herant's side of the bed was still empty. Half an hour later, he stumbled into bed.

"My God," he mumbled. "Wait till you hear . . ."

We had breakfast in the garden the next morning. Spring had come early that year, even for northern California, and the warm weather had coaxed the apricot into premature bloom. A hummingbird was zigzagging between the apricot and the blossoms of the lemon tree. Herant had half an hour before he had to teach a class at the university.

"What about the manuscript?" I asked.

"It's all very interesting and well written. She begins with the story of her family and really makes it come alive. She remembers all kinds of details. She writes fluently; everything flows.

"But suddenly, something happens. There is a chapter with the heading 'The First and the Last Time I Was in Love.' And you can tell she is writing under pressure. She makes mistakes, scratches words out. And she starts telling this love story. In great detail. I had no idea about any of this; I don't think anyone else had, either."

Herant shook his head in amazement. "It turns out she was in love with someone long before my father came along. She says she never stopped loving this man, even after she married my father."

Later that spring, Efronia developed stomach pains. Tests indicated gallstones, and her doctor recommended surgery.

The manuscript was sitting on Herant's desk, waiting to be translated. Efronia's secret hovered between us whenever we were together, but we never talked about it. I felt mildly embarrassed. It was as if my mother-in-law, at age ninety-two, had confessed that she had spent most of her life being pregnant, and now she had given birth.

We didn't quite know what to do with the baby.

In any case, the imminent operation gave us something else to think about. It was to be a fairly routine procedure, one week in the hospital, according to the doctor. But of course, with a patient her age, one never knew. There might be complications.

The afternoon of the operation, Herant phoned me from the hospital. His voice was choking. In the course of the operation, the surgeon had discovered a growth in the pancreas. They had done a biopsy.

The growth was malignant. It would be a matter of months.

While Efronia was in bed at home recuperating, Herant would go over to work with her on the translation of the manuscript into English.

I loved to watch them. The rustle of paper, the smell of fresh Turkish coffee, the sun coming in through the small back garden and making Efronia's hair, now back to its natural silver, shine like an angel's. Efronia's answers to Herant's questions were short and to the point.

More and more frequently, however, Efronia would abandon Armenian, the language she had always used with my husband, and lapse into Turkish. Efronia had been born in Turkey and had moved to Lebanon only in her mid-forties. Thus, she had lived half her life in a Turkish-speaking environment, and in the last months of her life, this was the language she returned to.

I understood only a few words of Turkish. But in these conversations, I could distinguish a name that kept coming up again and again.

Ramzi. From the look in Efronia's eyes, I knew this must have been her beloved.

Early in the fall, during that eerily quiet time on campus before the students return, Herant finished his translation of Efronia's manuscript.

By this time, Efronia had begun to wonder why it was taking her so long to recover from the gallbladder operation. No one had told her about the cancer, but we could see she was beginning to suspect that something was not right.

"I tell you," she said one day in her straightforward way, "I'm not going to get well from this. I'm going to die. And I'm ready."

I had just read her story. Silently, I was pleading for time. There was so much to talk about.

I wanted to ask her so many questions about the story. I wanted to tell her I finally understood why she had so readily accepted me, a foreigner, to be her son's wife.

All along, she had known that she and I shared a deep knowledge.

One time in her life, she had not used her head: a long time ago, she, too, had fallen in love with someone outside her own world.

2

Helsingfors to Beirut

"Armenian," I had written to my parents in Helsinki from Beirut. "He is Armenian. He is the most wonderful Armenian in the world. I am going to marry him."

My parents later told me they had looked up "Armenia" in *Nordisk Familjebok*, our frequently used family encyclopedia, which occupied the place of honor on our living room bookshelf.

"Aramaic . . . no . . . Armenian," mumbled my father, leafing through the pages. Then he cleared his throat and read aloud: "A very ancient people, with an advanced culture, who originally lived in the region known as Armenia, which comprised what is now northeastern Turkey and the Armenian Soviet Socialist Republic." He and my mother also learned that Armenian was the only surviving representative of a distinct branch of the Indo-European language family; that the Armenians had been the first nation to embrace Christianity, early in the fourth century; and that today Armenians numbered some six million, scattered all over the globe.

"I suppose this means that at least she won't have to wear a veil," said my father, in an effort to put a good face on this shattering piece of family news.

My sister was also in the room. They had called her over "for a glass of sherry." Doubtless, she knew something was up. Family news, good or bad, was always shared over a glass of sherry.

"I knew she would do something like this," exclaimed my sister, Maj, six years older than I. She sounded more excited than worried about this turn of events. She was the one who had urged me to go to Beirut in the first place, to visit a couple of good American friends at the American University of Beirut.

My sister thrives on drama. And those Armenians, ancient as well as modern, must have sounded pretty dramatic to her.

As a February snow flurry blurred the contours of the pines outside their window, my father filled the sherry glasses once more. Clearly, the ancient Armenians were of little concern to his younger daughter, who, according to what he could learn from her delirious letters from Beirut, had been met by this man at the airport and fallen in love with him on the way into the city. The feeling was apparently mutual, for she had accepted his proposal of marriage three weeks later.

The only pieces of hard information about their future son-in-law that they could glean from those gushing letters were that "he dances and skis like a god" and that he was a psychiatrist.

Not knowing whether to be relieved or alarmed by this last piece of information, they settled down to wait for the couple's arrival—two days before their wedding day—and to pray.

The six months in Beirut before my wedding were certainly enough to make me realize that I was about to marry into a community very different from my own but not different enough to deter me from going ahead with the marriage. And there was at least one important similarity of background that I shared with my future husband: both of us had grown up in a linguistic minority group.

For me, that group was the *finlandssvenskar*, or the Finland Swedes. For centuries, Finland had been part of Sweden, and over time, Swedish-speaking people had moved east and settled in the Finnish province. They became peasants and fishermen and educators and writers and captains of industry. At the time I was growing up, the Swedish-speaking population of Finland made up about ten percent of the total, and was far less integrated with the Finnish-speaking majority than it is now. I grew up in an almost totally Swedish-speaking world: I called my city *Helsingfors*, not Helsinki; I spoke Swedish with my friends, went to a school where Swedish was the language of instruction, listened to the radio in Swedish, wrote my schoolgirl poetry in Swedish and my first love letters, and knew by heart some of the poems of the Finnish poet Johan Ludvig Runeberg, who wrote in Swedish. Finnish was a language that was not part of my world, a language you studied in school and spoke in some shops and on buses and with people you didn't know.

In this sense, Finnish occupied very much the same place for me as Arabic did for my husband in Lebanon. He had taken Arabic at the Armenian school where he had studied, but he spoke it poorly, and most, if not all, of his social contacts were with other Armenians in the Lebanese Armenian community.

As members of linguistic minorities, we found many details of each other's lives amusingly familiar. One was both our families' enormous interest in family genealogy. A favorite topic of conversation both in Helsinki and in Beirut was the clarification of intricate family relationships over many generations. The conversations seemed identical—their frequency, their passion, their resemblance to a parlor game. In Finland, one of our relatives kept his genealogical reference works in the attic of his country home. He claimed that climbing the stairs to consult them was his only exercise. He was in very good shape.

These conversations, echoing each other in Swedish and Armenian, seemed driven by a similar urge: they felt like a collective effort to hold on to a community, to a way of life and a place in the universe, that was threatening to vanish for both our families.

But my new Armenian family seemed to be almost driven in their urge to keep bringing their long-lost family members back into the light of memory. Initially, this puzzled me.

Why this urgency?

Beirut in the early sixties was throbbing with the sort of frenetic pace that makes you wonder, in hindsight, if people didn't sense the impending disaster. The city was a feast for the senses—a peninsula jutting out into the blue Mediterranean, the pine-covered mountains with small villages on their slopes—but life was filled with tensions that seemed at the point of cracking the thin veneer of Western (mostly French) elegance that had made Beirut into a playground for those who liked their Orient with a European touch.

But for me, coming to Beirut was a little like entering a fortress. The fortress was my new family, several dozen of whom showed up to meet us at the Beirut airport when we returned from our Finnish wedding. The family functioned almost like the crusaders whose castles dotted the Lebanese and Syrian coasts: in good times, they were spread all over the city. But as soon as something happened—a funeral, a wedding, an illness, a celebration—they came streaming in from all directions to be together.

The first Armenian word I learned was *odar*. It means "foreign" and was used frequently in reference to me. It seemed to carry with it a cloud of meaning and a flavor I had not experienced before.

Finlanda meant as little to many of my new relatives as Armenia meant to my own family. *Finlanda*, *Irlanda*, they seemed to these new relatives to be lost in the northern bogs and mists, incomprehensible habitats for freezing human beings. *Yevrobatsi*, from Europe, was a little easier. But mostly, *odar* seemed definition enough, since it described what was essential: that I was not Armenian.

This word was not used in an unfriendly or exclusionary sense. Quite the contrary: the crusaders seemed eager to take me into their fortress, to include me within its walls. But even while I appreciated that openness and felt welcomed, I had a vague sense of being regarded as someone who was lacking in some essential way. Not personally, but in a very basic, ethnic sense. It wasn't what I was that was wrong. It was what I was not: *Hay*, the word Armenians use to refer to themselves.

If being referred to as an *odar* set me apart, then the second word used in reference to me connected me with the family and swept me up into the fortress. I was a *hars*.

"*Ays mer harsen eh*," Efronia announced, introducing me to the extended family during four evenings of receptions held at my in-laws' to celebrate our marriage. "This is our bride."

Nothing in my experience could have prepared me for all these relatives. It seemed as if the entire population of the city came pouring in during those humid, early September nights. The women, dressed, coiffed, and bejeweled, placed airy kisses on both my cheeks. The men shook my hand formally without making eye contact and then rapidly disappeared into a male enclave, Pepsis or whiskeys in hand.

And over all this presided Efronia, her hawk's eyes making sure that everyone had full glasses and plates heaped with food, her benevolent and tolerant spirit putting me at ease and making my foreignness less obvious.

The year I became Efronia's *hars* and she my *gesur-maeer* was the year that she turned seventy. But by sheer force of will and with the full cooperation of the whole extended family, she remained sixty-nine during the three years we lived in Beirut, and nobody seemed inclined to challenge her on that point.

In fact, challenging my mother-in-law on any point was not a light undertaking. She carried herself with an air of certainty that discouraged argument. "Your mother-in-law," someone once said to me, "could have commanded an army."

She had the self-possession and authority of beautiful women everywhere: Efronia had been extraordinarily beautiful when she was young. On the buffet in the dining room, against a wall covered with an Anatolian *kilim*, stood two photographs of her. One was a kindergarten picture. Efronia, four years old, is looking straight at the photographer with a pair of enormous, deep-set eyes. Compared with her focused self-awareness, the other children look like blurs.

The other photograph shows Efronia at eighteen. Her perfect oval of a face is surrounded by thick brown hair. She is not smiling. There is something urgent, almost pleading, mingled with the sweetness of her expression, something that comes from her heart and makes her look older than her years.

Initially, it was this photograph that made me wonder why she had married her husband. Granted, Aram, whom everyone addressed with the honorific title of *Effendi*, was a man with many endearing qualities and many admirable ones, as well. Ten years older than Efronia, he was a balding, thickset man with glasses, who by the time I entered the family had restricted his business life to a few minor projects and was spending a lot of time at home. He had strong opinions and would enforce them by raising his voice. Universally respected and sometimes even a little feared by people, he reminded me of an aging lion.

It was clear that he had been very successful in his younger years and that the life he and Efronia had led before coming to Beirut had been, by the standards of the day, a very glamorous one. Efronia frequently told stories about Iskenderun, the coastal town in Turkey where they had lived and where their son had been born. They had been one of the wealthiest Armenian families in the area and their social prominence had been such that, as Efronia put it, "when the *Catholicos*—the head of the Armenian Apostolic Church—came to town, he and his whole entourage would stay with us."

So maybe this was why she had married Aram Effendi—the predictability of life with a well-established businessman who clearly adored and respected her.

But even trying to imagine away forty-odd years from Aram Effendi's life, I still wondered why of all her many suitors, Efronia had chosen him for her husband. The eyes of that eighteen-year-old girl in the photograph, it seemed to me, were dreaming of more than social prominence and a dutiful husband.

Could it be that people thought differently about these things in this part of the world? That not every woman was looking for the perfect complement to the quirks of her own soul? That these things were, in fact, secondary to more pragmatic considerations: how their families would get along, what level of education the couple had attained, how well their temperaments were matched?

Efronia herself was a master of this kind of scrutiny, and people would often come to her for advice. She never hesitated to speak her mind after all the facts had been told to her regarding the young man's financial prospects; the couple's family backgrounds, including mental illness and physical handicaps that might be inherited; the chances of the young woman's being a good *dan digin*, a good housekeeper and mother. She would look for all-around compatibility and didn't want to leave much to chance. And when she had made up her mind, in these as well as other matters, it was either yes or no, black or white. There was no room for hesitation, vagueness, or diffuseness.

But something about the way she steered clear of the emotional considerations of matchmaking kept me wondering about her and Aram Effendi. Was there something she was hiding?

3

Food

On a beautiful spring morning in California, about a year after Efronia arrived, we went out for a ride up the winding old Page Mill Road into the hills that separate Palo Alto from the Pacific Ocean. Efronia enjoyed these rides and would often spend the time telling stories about her childhood in Aintab, later renamed Gaziantep, high on the Anatolian plateau in central Turkey—while constantly fishing out nuts and cookies and roasted sunflower seeds from her bottomless purse, "just a little something to change the taste in your mouth."

We parked next to a small lake in the hills. It was early in the morning, and no one was around. There was no wind, and the live oaks and the manzanitas were reflected perfectly in the water.

All of a sudden, down the trail came a deer and her fawn. The mother threaded her way carefully toward the water, a mere fifty feet from us. The fawn, fragile and graceful, followed her closely. Holding my breath at the beauty of the scene, I felt Efronia stirring next to me.

"Aaah," she said, "the little one. They are very tasty. Now, you take a few onions, some garlic . . ."

Where I grew up, food was de-emphasized. It was not good form to talk too much about it or to take too much pleasure in it. Eating was regarded as just another bodily necessity. You didn't ask what was for dinner and you didn't comment on the food. You put it in your mouth, you ate slowly and with restraint, you watched your table manners, and you thought and talked about loftier things.

I was ill prepared for the onslaught of Armenian food, and even worse prepared to understand the central place of *geragur* in the world of my mother-in-law.

The Anatolian plateau of Central Turkey is a rugged country with hot summers and very cold winters, and the soil is often rocky and hard to work. But with the limited variety of grains and vegetables available to them, the Armenians had developed a cuisine as delicious as it was healthy. They reveled in their food, placed it at the center of human interaction, and made its offering a sign of love.

Efronia came from a family famous for its cooks, and even in her later life she was an undisputed master. Everyone agreed that no one could make *kuftes* as elastic and delicate as hers, open up the dough for a *sou beureg* to such thinness, or prepare tastier *sarmas* in vine-leaf wrappers. It was also generally agreed that with Efronia at the head of the table, you'd better start saying no before she had even started serving you, or else you would never get through the seven-course dinner. Not many people got through all the courses, even with Efronia's constant exhortations: *"Ger, ger!* Eat, eat!" It was always a moment of triumph for Efronia to appear at the head of the table with the last course, only to be chased back into the kitchen with it again to the accompaniment of everybody's protests and groans.

She had won.

In family lore, food and eating occupied center stage. I sometimes amused myself by trying to imagine my own mother giving an account of what she had eaten at someone's house thirty years before: she wouldn't have noticed, much less remembered. In my new family, on the other hand, food played a big role in their stories.

"When I was seven years old," Efronia would say, "we went to visit my aunt Arpine. It was a freezing cold evening, and there was a blizzard. We almost lost our way in the dark, but at last we found her house. She had prepared stuffed peppers."

People were sometimes identified by how much they could eat. "My cousin Hagop, who once ate twenty *lahmejuns* . . ." The legendary eaters occupied a special place in the family stories.

Efronia knew a hundred ways in which to trick people into eating. We lived outside Beirut, in a lovely mountain village called Beit Meri, half an hour's drive away. Occasionally, after some late-night affair, we would sleep at my in-laws' in town to avoid the drive. They would have gone to bed by the time we got to their home, but without fail we would find the hallway, the living room through which we had to pass, and the bedroom itself strewn with small bowls of food: a plate of cookies here, some nuts and sunflower seeds there, string cheese, raisins, dried figs, halvah.

Just in case we got hungry before breakfast.

And at breakfast, when Efronia appeared, the interrogation would begin. *Inch gerak?* What did you eat? And when I was through with the description of the menu and the order of the courses, Efronia would pass judgment. A good hostess would get an approving smile: "I knew she would serve a good dinner." A bad one, and Efronia's hands would fly into the air, palms up, shoulders lifted, a gesture of incomprehension and profound disbelief.

Efronia never approved of the much simpler eating habits she encountered in California (although she developed some strange enthusiasms, freeze-dried coffee and Spam among them). Some of my friends will never know how many times I salvaged their reputations in my mother-in-law's eyes by adding imaginary dishes to their dinners. Once, in an unguarded moment, I made the mistake of confessing that I'd been to a luncheon at the home of a high university official, a "spouses' lunch," and that it was an informal, brown-bag meeting.

"What did you eat?"

"Well, we all brought our own lunches in paper bags. And then there was tea and coffee and . . ."

"You brought your *own* lunches? What kind of invitation was that?"

I knew it was useless. Efronia never forgot who had given that brown-bag lunch.

I have a black notebook on my kitchen shelf in which I've gathered Armenian recipes handed down by Efronia. Some are from Beirut, from the time before she realized that the complexities of my life made it quite unlikely I would ever use them. "Yes, it takes time," she would say. "But you know, it is very nice. You gather your friends, you all sit around, you wrap the rice filling in the grape leaves, and you talk . . ."

In California she realized she would have to make some adaptations. She made them with the skill of a musician transposing a piece of music to another key. She would not compromise. There had to be a flour that would make as good a dough for *beureg* as the kind she used in Beirut. A shortening as versatile as Vegetalin. A cut of meat for *chee kufte* (meatballs) as fine as her Beirut butcher's. She searched, she asked, she sniffed, she experimented, and, finally, she succeeded.

When she was satisfied, dishes of food started going in all directions: to a neighbor, the butcher, a distant relative in

Detroit, her grandchild in college, the postman, the plumber. Even to relatives in Finland, if our flight was non-stop.

I'll never forget sitting through a matinee at the Metropolitan Opera in New York with a package of *lahmejuns* and *kuftes* destined for friends in Connecticut under my seat and wondering when the aroma of Armenian food was going to stop the performance. Or meeting Efronia at Heathrow Airport the year we were on sabbatical in England and seeing her wobble through customs like a tank without being asked to open a single one of her huge bags bursting with smuggled food. Or the despair of my husband when he discovered that she had escaped from the civil war in Beirut carrying with her not the family albums or some other irreplaceable object, but pistachio nuts, dried figs, raisins, and dates, which she knew we liked.

There was enough deprivation and hunger in Efronia's early life to make it easy to understand why she would later want to feed the world around her. Even late in her final illness, when she herself was reduced to a diet of yogurt and baby food, she would perk up at the mention of some intriguing dish. In one of her last conversations with Lucine, she extracted a promise from her to "cook for Herant and his family after I'm gone."

And I'm convinced that, if there is a heaven and if she and I are lucky enough to meet each other there, she will greet me by saying: "Oh, by the way, I just happened to find some very fine eggplant. You will like this for dinner tomorrow. . . ."

4

Shadows

I learned my Armenian as a child learns a language, by using my ears. Armenian has its own ancient alphabet, invented by the monk Mesrop Mashtots in the fifth century A.D. I was convinced the fastest way to understand what people around me were saying was to listen and ask questions. Gradually, the words swirling around me began to make sense. To aid my memory I made my own little Armenian-Swedish "dictionary" and invented my own spellings of what I heard. It's an odd little book, but it did the trick: the sounds began to carry meaning, and the Armenian world in which I lived slowly came into focus.

The boisterous dinners in Beirut with the extended family often ended in evenings of storytelling and high spirits. One after another, members of the family would recall practical jokes, blunders, and pranks of their relatives, living and deceased. There was a slapstick, uproarious quality to the stories but also an underlying sadness.

The more Armenian I understood, the more I realized that something was missing from the family members' lives. They were always looking back, back to the past, trying to find it.

I was puzzled. It seemed as if a whole world, somewhere, had ceased to exist. Everyone in the Armenian community was uprooted, everyone was from somewhere else, and people referred to each other that way: "He is from Urfa. *Urfatsi.*"

From Kharput. From Marash. From Zeitoun. From Sassoun. From Adana. From Erzerum. From Bitlis.

From all over the Turkish provinces of Central and Eastern Anatolia.

"His uncle was a pharmacist in Hadjin."

"She went to the girls' seminary in Aintab."

"His father was a shoemaker in Kilis."

"He and his two brothers were stonemasons in Bursa."

They were teachers and peasants and jewelers and black-smiths; clergymen and doctors and merchants and nurses; weavers and dressmakers. They owned land and they farmed it. They went to church and they married; they had children and they died.

There was a sense of continuity and of history and of deep ties to the land. But then that land was gone, and everyone was suddenly from somewhere else.

In the stories I was hearing, one word kept recurring—*Turkere*, the Turks—and a date—1915.

Slowly, my awareness of a distant catastrophe that had befallen the Armenian people began to crystallize. Though still nebulous in my mind, the catastrophe seemed like a collective nightmare, as unreal as the mythical Kingdom of Nairi from which the Armenians are said to have descended.

And then, in 1965, there were great stirrings in the Armenian community worldwide. There were protests and meetings, and I understood this was the fiftieth anniversary of a great calamity.

It was then that Efronia, perhaps to show me that the Armenians had long led a precarious existence in the Ottoman Empire, told me the story of her father.

"I never knew my father," she said one day as we were wrapping grape leaves around rice filling for *sarma*. "He died when I was only two months old. At age twenty-nine, my mother was left a widow with five children."

"How did he die, Mama?"

Efronia took a bunch of leaves from the jar and started removing the stalks. The joints of her fingers were knotted with arthritis. Suddenly, there was a weariness in the movement of her hands.

"Let me tell you how it happened, *aghchigs*," she said.

"My father was a shoe merchant. They say he was very handsome. When he went to work in the morning, Turkish women used to stand at their windows to catch a glimpse of him.

"My father owned two stores in the Aintab bazaar, which was only a few blocks away from us. We lived in the Turkish quarter, in a house that my grandfather had built. In one of the stores, my father sold materials for making shoes, and in the other, he had workers who made shoes. At that time, there were no ready-made shoes. If you wanted shoes, you either had to go to a store like my father's to have your feet measured, or you had the shoemaker come to your house.

"Several times a year, my father used to travel to Aleppo to purchase materials for his stores. At the end of October 1895, he was again going to make the trip. These were tense times, and people told him not to go, but he insisted on going.

" 'Then keep your money in cash,' they said. 'You never know what will happen.'

"The Turks and the Armenians had been living together in these parts for hundreds of years—mostly peacefully. We had many Turkish friends, and we spoke Turkish most of the time. My mother didn't know any Armenian at all. It wasn't until my generation that we began learning Armenian in school.

"Still, my parents knew that things could flare up any time and that the Armenians had to be very careful.

"Nevertheless, my father went to Aleppo and came back with three hundred gold sovereigns' worth of materials for his store. By the time he got back, the political situation in town was very tense, and many Armenians were staying at home."

Efronia started spreading small amounts of rice filling on the grape leaves and wrapping them up into tight, finger-shaped bundles.

"Close to our house lived a Turkish mufti," she continued, "a Moslem religious judge who liked my father and who often ordered shoes from him.

"One morning, my mother told my father: 'Kevork, last night the light in the *selamlik*—the mufti's reception room— was on all night. I wonder what was keeping him up.' As my mother was saying this, Mehdin, the mufti's son, came over to our house and told my father: 'Kevork Agha, my father wants you to come to our house right away.' But my father told Mehdin he had some errands to run in the bazaar and that he would be over later. As soon as the boy left, he told my mother: 'I know what it's about. The mufti is going to order another pair of shoes. He hasn't paid for the last two pairs. I'm not going.'

"The mufti was very upset when he realized my father had left for the bazaar. He told his son to run after him and tell him to come back at once. The boy did as he was told, but my father just waved him off."

Efronia stopped and wiped her hands on her apron.

"The reason the mufti wanted to see my father was to warn him there was going to be a massacre of Armenians. But my father wouldn't listen. And that was the last chance my father had to save himself. Later, my mother often used to say that he had sought his own death.

"He continued on down to the bazaar. It was a busy Saturday morning, with people milling about in the narrow streets. He had started to select some green peppers for pickling to take to his sister-in-law, when a disturbance broke out. All of a sudden, he was surrounded by a mob of Turks. We never found out quite how it happened. But a man attacked him with an ax and killed him.

"The assailant was a butcher by the name of Abdul. He chopped my father's head off. And after that, the mob looted both his stores.

"When this happened, *rahmetlik Babas*, my blessed father, was thirty-five years old."

Efronia looked at me. "The massacre began in the morning and lasted late into the night. The previous night, people had marked the doors of the Armenians who lived in the Moslem quarter—and then they came for them. We were saved because the mufti had issued strict orders not to harm anyone on our street."

Efronia was arranging the *sarmas* in neat layers in the pot. There was a small amount of rice filling left, and she asked me to prepare a few more grape leaves.

"My mother told me I cried a lot when I was a baby, after my father was killed. Sometimes my crying could be heard all the way to the mufti's house, and he would send word to my mother with one of his three wives to please stop my crying. He could not bear to listen to it, knowing how I had become an orphan."

"What happened to the butcher who killed your father, Mama? Was he ever punished?" I asked. I found it hard to let go of the notion that somehow justice would prevail in the end.

"He did not live long. He was taken ill and brought to a hospital where my cousin was the chief surgeon. After the operation, my cousin bent over him and whispered into his ear: 'I could have saved your life, Abdul, but I didn't. You

27

killed my uncle with your ax, and now you are going to die yourself.' "

Efronia closed the lid on the pot full of *sarmas*.

"The butcher never made it home from the hospital."

Sultan Abdul Hamid II—the instigator of the massacres of 1894–1896, which killed Efronia's father, along with several hundred others in Aintab alone—was a disaster for the Ottoman Empire. The "Red Sultan," as he was called, was a paranoid man of mediocre intelligence who corrupted his government and demoralized his people. The sultan's spies were everywhere; it was said that wherever three people were talking, it was certain that one of them was a spy. The sultan took to receiving people with a small child on his lap to ensure that no one would murder him. His paranoia touched every aspect of life. He is said to have banned performances of *Macbeth, Hamlet, Julius Caesar*, and any other play in which a prince or a leader was killed, so that no one would get the wrong idea.

Despite a certain cunning, Abdul Hamid did no better in foreign policy than he did at home. During his long reign, Ottoman Turkey lost Bulgaria, Crete, the area around Kars in the east, Tunis, and Tripoli. Turkey, the sick man of Europe, had never looked worse.

Abdul Hamid's brutal tactics alienated the many minorities living in his vast empire. He showed particular hatred toward the Armenians, attacking the ancient privileges of the Armenian churches and imposing a variety of crushing taxes. Armenian schools were closed on the slightest pretext, the Armenian language was suppressed, people were thrown in jail without trial.

In the light of things to come, of course, the massacres of

1894–1896 were later looked upon as merely an attempt by Sultan Abdul Hamid II "to teach the Armenians a lesson."

And despite the early tragedy of her father's death, Efronia always thought of her childhood in Aintab as a very happy time. She had one remarkable woman in particular to thank for those happy memories: her mother, Ovsannah.

5

Aintab

By the time he was nineteen, Efronia's handsome father had been well established in his shoemaking business. It was time for him to get married. His parents had been looking for a suitable match for some time, and now they thought they had found her. Her name was Ovsannah. She was the beautiful daughter of Hagop Matossian, a well-off businessman, and his much younger wife, Trvandah, famous in all of Aintab for her green eyes.

Ovsannah had lived a sheltered childhood, even by the standards of the day. The Matossians had lost their only other child, a son, two years before Ovsannah was born. They took no chances with Ovsannah: to prevent her from getting sick, they kept her at home. A private tutor came regularly to teach her how to read the Bible, the only book she was allowed to read, and she learned large parts of it by heart. She also learned to cook and sew, to spin, and to embroider, skills she would put to good use later in life, as a young widow with five children to raise.

Kevork's parents arranged for a series of visits to meet the Matossians and to see Ovsannah. Following custom, the conversations between the two couples touched on neutral matters; Hagop Matossian might have talked about his business of importing kerosene from Iskenderun, Hagop Nazarian might have found an opportunity to mention how well his son

Kevork's business was going, and when the conversation was well under way, young Ovsannah obliged them by silently coming into the room with a tray of Turkish coffee and some sweets.

It was all she needed to do. After one of the visits, Kevork's parents told their son: "We have found the right girl for you. She is the Matossians' only daughter. They are a good family and quite wealthy, and their daughter, Ovsannah, is very beautiful."

Kevork didn't hesitate. "You may ask for her hand. I want to marry her."

Kevork's parents may have been a little surprised by his eagerness. They didn't know he had followed them on one of their visits to the Matossians. Once he knew which house they lived in, it was only a matter of time before he caught a glimpse of young Ovsannah.

"And once he saw her, he fell in love with her," Efronia told me once. "But my poor father had to promise to wait five years before marrying her. Ovsannah was only fourteen at the time. Her own mother, Trvandah, had been married at thirteen, and they had realized that marrying so young was a mistake."

The parents, having agreed on a waiting period of five years, decided the young couple should get engaged right away. "At that time," said Efronia, "the young couple couldn't see each other, even at the engagement party. The girl stayed in her house, the boy in his. But these two families were not so ignorant and conservative. They decided the engagement rings would be exchanged in Ovsannah's house, in the presence of close relatives."

That was the first time Ovsannah laid eyes on her future husband. "Once my father saw my mother up close," said Efronia, "those five years seemed like a very long time. He was permitted to visit my mother's parents, and eventually he persuaded them to allow him to see his fiancée for a few minutes each time—but only in their presence."

At the end of the five years, Ovsannah, equipped with a large dowry, was given a lavish wedding that was the talk of the Aintab community for years to come. The festivities lasted for eight days, during which Ovsannah's hands and fingernails were painted with henna, presents were exchanged to the accompaniment of dancing and singing, and banquets were held every night. On the day of the wedding ceremony, Ovsannah was given an exquisitely embroidered veil by her husband, and then, accompanied by musicians and dancing, ululating women, the candlelit wedding procession wound its way to the church. After Kevork and Ovsannah emerged from the church, a sheep was slaughtered at their feet in celebration, and to the cheers of the crowd, Kevork picked Ovsannah off the ground and stepped over the sheep.

The meat of that sheep was given to the poor. Ovsannah, sheltered daughter of wealthy parents, in the arms of her handsome husband, surrounded by gifts and by an Armenian community whose roots went back to the time of the crusades, was looking at a rosy future.

In Ovsannah's world—and later, in Efronia's, as well—the Armenian Evangelical Church was the center of people's lives. By the time Efronia was growing up, it had grown from a fledgling Protestant congregation in the 1850s—started and initially run by American Protestant missionaries—into a church of nearly four thousand members, two thousand of whom attended Sunday services regularly. More than once, when Efronia became of marriageable age, Ovsannah turned down requests for her daughter's hand because the suitor was "from the wrong church." How, after all, could she allow her daughter to marry a man from the Armenian Apostolic or the Armenian Catholic Church?

One of the reasons Ovsannah felt so loyal to the Evangelical Church was its emphasis on education. She herself had not been allowed to go to school; she would see to it that her children didn't suffer the same fate. Around the turn of the century, it seemed as if every conceivable form of education had taken root in the Protestant community of Aintab. There were kindergartens, Sunday schools, a teacher-training institute, efforts to establish a museum and a library, several educational associations for women, programs to bring education to the poor, a book club for women, and even an evening school that offered a variety of classes, including English, and didn't have nearly enough room for all the students who wanted to attend.

Kevork and Ovsannah's first child was a son. The called him Yacoub. After him, in rapid succession, came two girls, Aroussiak and Azniv; then another boy, Yervant. Efronia, the last-born, was only two months old when Kevork was killed in the bazaar. Meanwhile, Ovsannah's father had lost all his money.

Ovsannah's long years of struggle had begun. First, she began to sell her jewelry and the more valuable pieces of her dowry. Then she sold some of the family's furniture. She patched her children's clothing and then put patches on the patches. She forbade her children to wear shoes indoors, so that the shoes would last longer. She took in work, washing clothes and mending the underwear and socks of the students at the local college.

When all of that wasn't enough to make ends meet, Ovsannah went to the church and asked to become a "Bible woman." She visited poor families and patients in the hospital and read the Bible to them, earning a little money from each visit. With her monthly earnings, Efronia tells us, she bought "half a liter of olive oil, a bag of charcoal, and a bag of firewood, which were essential things. And with the rest, she had to take care of our other needs—but she had difficulty making ends meet. She could buy meat only twice a month."

Some relatives helped them. One of Efronia's cousins bought them their store of bulgur wheat for the winter. Another relative bought them their cheese, and a third helped with the clothing. And one relative took special care of Yacoub's needs. As the oldest son, he had to get ahead in the world so that he would be in a position to help his family in turn.

"Yet in the midst of all these difficulties," writes Efronia, "my mother still tried to keep us happy. And in fact, we lived quite happily with each other, satisfied with the little we had. She would often tell us about the poor people she visited and ask that we thank God for the warm meals we had, while those poor people had nothing to put on their bread but grape leaves sprinkled with salt. And when we asked her for something, she would never say, 'Where shall I get it from? You have no father; don't ask for such things.' Instead, she would use gentle words, saying, 'Don't be sad. I will get it for you one day.' We would wait patiently, and she would usually get us what we wanted sooner or later. We were a happy family. Many times, neighbors would come to us and ask, 'You, who are so poor, how come you laugh so much?' "

Ovsannah could have made life easier for herself if she had let her sons apprentice themselves to local artisans and earn some money while they were learning a trade. But she had larger ambitions for them, and she sent both of them to the men's college in Aintab.

In the spring of 1912, as Ovsannah sat in the First Church of Aintab, watching Efronia receive her high school diploma, she felt her years of struggle were finally over. Her older daughters had married well-to-do husbands; her younger son, Yervant, had two years to go in the local men's college; Efronia, shining like a jewel among the young women in white dresses, was graduating at the top of her class. Ovsannah had no worries about Efronia. Beautiful, intelligent, and much beloved by all her teachers, she had never caused Ovsannah any trouble. And here she was, giving the valedictory address on "The Progress of Women through the Ages." Next year, God willing, she would enroll in the women's college in nearby Marash. And after she graduated, it would only be a matter of choosing the most suitable of all the young men who were already asking for her hand. Yes, Ovsannah thought as the organ started up and the graduates were filing out of the church, Efronia would be no problem for her.

She looked at her elder son, Yacoub, seated next to her, and squeezed his hand. Yacoub had been her problem child. But now he, too, seemed to be heading toward a good future. A few days before Efronia's graduation, Ovsannah, to her immense joy, had learned that Yacoub had been admitted to pharmacy school at the top institution of higher learning in all of the Ottoman Empire: the Syrian Protestant College of Beirut.

Looking at her handsome son, she tried hard to forget the despair he had caused her the year before.

6

A Bee Sting

Even when he was a young boy, Ovsannah could see that her first-born son, Yacoub, was going to be a problem child. He had a volatile temper that she ascribed to the shock of losing his father at such an early age—Yacoub had been nine years old then—and being thrust into the position of man of the family much too early. Ovsannah tried to compensate by giving Yacoub special attention: she cooked him a special dinner with meat on his birthdays, favored him over the others when it came to clothes and shoes, gave him extra presents whenever she could.

Yacoub reacted to all this by demanding even more of her and by showing little understanding of the family's financial circumstances. He loved spending money on himself and showed little inclination to share his earnings with his family. But Ovsannah didn't lose hope: she persisted in gently pushing Yacoub down the educational path.

One day, during Yacoub's second year of college in Aintab, Ovsannah got a message from the school.

Yacoub was in serious trouble.

Efronia's memoirs describe the situation thus:

One day, my mother was called to the college and told that her son was going to be expelled. He had a very bad companion named

Haroutune. Together they had stolen a violin from the college, sold it, and divided up the money. Their friends had learned about the theft and told the headmaster. Yacoub and his friend were forced to confess the truth.

After hearing this news, my mother returned home with my brother, who was crying and wailing. I will never forget that day. She scolded him and berated him, but what good would it do? What was done, was done. My mother appealed, begged, and pleaded with many people, but to no avail. Then my aunt's son, Professor Levonian, intervened. They took him back and he finished college.

But the incident left grave doubts in Ovsannah's mind about Yacoub. Could she really rely on him to help them in the future? Were her sacrifices on his behalf doomed to come to naught?

Ovsannah decided to trust in God and hope for the best. With the money from the sale of furniture that belonged to her mother, Trvandah, she packed Yacoub off to Beirut and to pharmacy school.

This, she hoped, might be the turning point for him.

Yacoub was very happy at the institution, which was later to become the American University of Beirut. He wrote home regularly with good news: his studies were going well, and he was popular with the other students. He earned money waiting tables in the cafeteria of one of the dormitories, which also allowed him to eat for free.

Ovsannah was delighted. Her elder son seemed a changed man. He even expressed his gratitude to her in his letters.

She pushed her remaining doubts about him out of her mind. When Yacoub, soon after graduation, accepted an offer to run a newly opened pharmacy in the small coastal town of Iskenderun, she was overjoyed.

This was truly an excellent opportunity, Ovsannah thought.

God had answered her prayers. Yacoub's job carried the prospect of full partnership, and his employers were three brothers from a family in Aintab that was related to her by marriage: Sarkis, Yeghia, and Aram Katchadourian.

There had actually been six Katchadourian brothers (some were long dead), and they had always been an enterprising lot. Their grandfather, the founder of the clan, a formidable man by the name of Khatchadour, had been the head of what amounted to a small commercial fiefdom in the area around Aintab. The old man owned several villages and traded in copper far and wide, and it was said that it took ninety donkeys to carry the produce from his lands. One of his sons, Adour, had married four times and fathered six sons and six daughters.

One of Efronia's cousins, Marie, was married to Yeghia, the third youngest of Adour's sons. It was Marie who provided the family link between the Katchadourian brothers in Iskenderun and the newly graduated pharmacist Yacoub Nazarian.

Everyone in Efronia's family was pleased that Yacoub would be working in the brothers' pharmacy. After a few weeks of preparation, Yacoub said a tearful farewell to his family and set out for Iskenderun.

The initial news from there was good. Yacoub wrote immediately to say that he had been met by Yeghia and his wife, Marie, on the outskirts of the town and that he had stayed with them until he had found a nice room to rent. The day after his arrival, the Katchadourians had taken him over to the new pharmacy and handed him the keys.

"Here it is, Yacoub," they told him. "Treat this pharmacy as your own. If you take good care of the business, we will make you a full partner after a while."

For several months, Yacoub wrote regularly. Each month,

39

he sent his mother money. It was not much, but it was sufficient, and Ovsannah remained hopeful.

But after Yacoub had been in Iskenderun a year, the monthly sum of money started shrinking, and the letters came less frequently. Ovsannah was worried; one day, she got a letter from the Katchadourians that confirmed her worst fears.

They had seen it coming for some time, they said. Yacoub was consorting with loose women. He was gambling. He was missing work. Still, they had preferred to say nothing to Ovsannah. They were very fond of her and were well aware of the difficulties she had been through. Finally, however, they had gone to the pharmacy to check the books. They were shocked. The pharmacy was in the red. Yacoub had been living far beyond his means, and the money to support his shady lifestyle had been coming out of the pharmacy's revenues.

The Katchadourian brothers were outraged. They gave him one warning, then another. Finally, when they were about to throw him out, the women in the family pleaded for a compromise: Ask Ovsannah, her mother, Trvandah, and her daughter Efronia to come and live in Iskenderun as soon as school was out. Maybe Yacoub simply was not ready to be completely on his own.

For Yacoub, this was a humiliating development. But the request was made, and it presented Ovsannah with a difficult choice.

Her second son, Yervant, still had one more year to finish college: what would become of him and her two older daughters, who were also living in Aintab? Yet she felt she had no alternative.

Efronia writes:

She thought about it a good deal but she had no alternative. I recall her saying, "We used to live better when we were dependent on the help of others and on my earnings than after my son became a pharmacist." And she was quite right, because we were again in financial difficulties. Those who had been helping us ceased to do so, thinking our problems were over. My mother had thanked them and expressed her gratitude to them many times over, saying she would not forget their goodness for the rest of her life. She had also stopped working. Yet the money my brother was now sending us was not enough to live on. So what else could she do but move to where he was?

And so it was that Efronia, one month after graduating from high school, left her home town and set out on the road to Iskenderun, to fall in love "for the first and only time," as she would put it.

Iskenderun (or Alexandretta) was a bustling harbor town on the Bay of Iskenderun, in the extreme northeastern corner of the Mediterranean. To the East lay the Amanos coastal range, where a pass, the Syrian Gates, gave access to the interior. It had never really been a great city, but it had held its own down through the centuries as a starting point for inland commerce.

As Efronia writes,

*In those days one traveled either by mule or by covered wagons—*yayle araba—*which were drawn by two or three horses. There was a coachman in Aintab called Mule Driver Hagop. Apparently the Katchadourians knew him well and had suggested to my brother that he arrange for this man to take us to Iskenderun himself. A trustworthy person, he owned a number of wagons and employed several coachmen. His house in Aintab was far from us, but one evening he came to our house and showed us the letters he had received from the Katchadourians and my brother.*

Chapter 6

"Get yourselves ready," he told my mother. "In a few days, I will take you to Iskenderun. I promised your son I would personally drive your wagon, although I don't ordinarily do this sort of work anymore."

The journey would take five days. The roads were not safe. There were no hotels on the way, and we would have to spend the night in local khans *(inns). I was a young and attractive woman.*

We started early one morning. We spent the first night in Sareyarek, the second night in Kilis, the third night in Afrin, and the fourth night in Kirikhan. The coachman hardly slept for four nights. Instead, he kept guard all night by sitting in a chair in front of our door in the khan. *I sensed he was trying to keep me out of sight.*

During the day, we had all our meals inside the wagon, and we could also take naps there on some bedding and a few pillows.

Occasionally the coachman would fall asleep in the driver's seat, and the horses would stop moving. We would have to wake him up in order to get going again.

The road was dusty and bumpy, and the closer to the coast they got, the more humid it became. Efronia thought she would suffocate inside the covered wagon. With each creaking mile away from Aintab, her anxiety was growing: what was this new place going to be like? How long was she going to have to stay there? She would be eighteen soon; many of her classmates were going on to the women's college in Marash, and here she was, confined to a hot wagon with two old women.

Efronia tried hard to suppress her resentment toward her brother.

Their last lunch stop was by a meadow full of shade trees, off the road sloping down toward Iskenderun. Efronia got out of the wagon as fast as she could, and while Ovsannah placed a couple of blankets in the shade and unpacked their lunch, she ran all the way to the edge of the meadow. Far below her, in a distant bluish haze, lay the Mediterranean. Almost against her will, Efronia felt excited. So much water! It looked to her like a giant, blank sheet of paper.

Reaching down to pick a flower, she felt a sharp sting on the tip of her middle finger. She screamed. Mule Driver Hagop came running. The finger hurt and was beginning to swell up. Ovsannah tried to comfort her, while Hagop ran for help to the village nearby. Eventually, a man came and squeezed some blood out of the finger and applied an ointment.

Seventy years later, Efronia recalled this incident in her memoir. She wondered what it might mean, this poisonous sting, the day before she arrived in Iskenderun.

Efronia believed in omens.

Late that afternoon, they arrived at her cousin Marie's house. The exhausted coachman, enormously relieved, told them this was the last time he would ever consent to being in charge of a traveling party that included an attractive young woman. They had some kebabs for supper and drank their coffee, and then they started to unpack.

While they were unpacking, Efronia noticed that her brother and a friend of his, a young man who had come to help, were constantly whispering to each other. Ovsannah turned to Yacoub and asked what they were saying.

"Oh, Mother," Yacoub said, "promise you won't be upset. The Turks have declared war on the Bulgarians, and they are recruiting soldiers from all over. I have been called to duty as a pharmacist. So I must leave for the front in a week."

Ovsannah turned to Efronia. "Stop unpacking. I am not staying here one minute longer. I want to return to Aintab."

"But, Mother, you have rented our house to someone else.

43

Where will we stay if we return? How will we manage? We have to stay here. There's no other way."

"My dear Lord," Ovsannah sighed, "has my journey to Golgotha not ended yet?"

Three days after Ovsannah, Efronia, and Trvandah had arrived in Iskenderun, Yacoub put on his officer's uniform and left them for the Balkans. The August heat was at its worst. The town was a hothouse, day and night. To escape it, people had gone up to one of the nearby mountain villages: Sovouk Olük, Nargizlik, Jizmeli, where the air was dry and the evenings cool.

But Efronia, her mother, and her grandmother, newcomers in Iskenderun with limited means, were forced to stay in town. Efronia, her finger still swollen from the bee sting, finished unpacking the day after her brother left for the war.

Two Suitors

"Aghchigs," Efronia used to say, "my daughter, beauty has brought me more trouble than it's been worth—and caused more misery for other poor souls than I can ever tell you."

She might have been thinking of what happened soon after she arrived that summer in Iskenderun. She wanted a job badly; the days at home alone with her mother and grandmother were intolerably long. After inquiries, she discovered an Armenian elementary school that needed a part-time teacher. She was offered the job, but before taking it she had to secure Ovsannah's permission.

That was no easy matter, but after many tears and pleadings Ovsannah relented. She agreed that Efronia had a point: It was preferable that Efronia put her education to good use rather than stay home all day and be unhappy. Efronia started teaching second-grade mathematics and Armenian history, and Ovsannah settled down uneasily to see what would happen when her beautiful daughter began to walk about the town, unescorted and in full daylight. Most of all, she feared what Yacoub would say once he returned from the war.

She didn't have to wait long. After an absence of two months, Yacoub was back, and his reaction was predictable:

"Me! Going to let my sister work? Impossible!"

It took several people and a flood of Efronia's tears to

persuade him that her working didn't reflect badly on him as
a provider. She wasn't working for the money, they pointed
out; she just wanted to be useful to the community. Finally,
Yacoub relented. But the ensuing calm didn't last very long,
as Efronia observes:

*My mother's predictions began to come true. Young men from all
around started to pursue me. Fears began to fill my mother's heart.
But she had a lot of trust in me. I hadn't given any thought to all
the young men who had been after me ever since I was very young. I
had no desire to get married at that time. I was a confident and
courageous girl, not one to be fooled easily. I had high moral
standards and I was, as they say, the owner of my own beauty. All
I wanted was to get better educated.*

*Very soon, several young men came forth with marriage proposals.
Two of them were not Armenian; we refused them outright, and they
gave up. But two other suitors were another matter. One of them was
related to my mother; his name was Setrak. The other one was my
brother's closest friend, Mihran.*

*Setrak and his mother looked after us like guardian angels while
my brother was away in the war. And I very much regret that the
love and respect he showed me became the cause of his unhappiness. He
began to court me, tried to get close to me, and brought me presents.
When I sensed this, I tried to stay away and changed the times when
I came home from school.*

*One day he told my mother that he wanted to marry me. My
mother knew very well that I felt no love for him. Nevertheless, she
promised to ask me. When she did, I said, "Don't ever speak to me
about this again. It is impossible. I neither love him nor enjoy his
company."*

*My mother kept quiet. I added, "If you cannot say this to him
yourself, I will personally tell him to his face." I sensed that my
mother was favorably disposed toward him; he was related to us, and*

he was not a bad young man. But she knew I didn't want to marry him, and on his next visit she tried gently to persuade him to give up the matter. Setrak was beside himself and begged for an opportunity to speak to me personally and to express his love for me.

He came, and we spoke at length. I first thanked him for the love and respect he had shown and all he had done to help us during my brother's absence. Then I added, "I don't want to deceive you by pretending affection. I love you as a brother, as a relative, but not as a future husband. If you continue to come to our house, come as a relative and not with the intention of marriage. Otherwise, although I truly like you, you must stop coming to us as of this moment."

Poor Setrak did what any young man would have done under the circumstances. He begged Efronia to think it over. He tried to persuade her with what Efronia refers to as "lavish promises and sweet words," but to no avail. Finally, he left and didn't show up for several weeks.

Mihran was a tougher case, Efronia recalls:

The house where Mihran lived was on the way to my school. Every morning when I passed by, Mihran would stand there and look at me until I turned the corner. But I went on my way without greeting him or looking at him.

A number of times, I took another, longer way to school, but it was only a matter of time before he began to show up along that route, as well. Not once did I encourage him to approach me, to open his heart to me, or to explain his reason for pursuing me. Finally, he was obliged to send his parents over to see us.

The day they announced their visit, my mother sent word to my brother to be home that evening. At that time, my brother was quite unconcerned about us. He had no idea of my predicament. Many nights a week, he would not come home until morning, and then he

47

would go directly to the pharmacy. When we needed money, we had to go there to ask for it.

That night, however, my brother came home, and we had dinner together. After a while the guests arrived: Mihran's parents, his older sister, and her husband. We knew why they had come, so after serving coffee, I withdrew to my room. They then revealed the purpose of their visit, and after some discussion, my mother told them, "You are always welcome at our house, and we thank you for your visit. But give us some time. We have just gotten to know each other. Let us think the matter over, and we will let you know." As they were leaving, I came out and bade them farewell.

After they left, my brother said, "These people, particularly their son, got it into their heads to propose to you before you even came here. Mihran had seen your picture in my room. The day you arrived, even though his family was at their mountain resort, he came to town to be with me when I met you. Although he is not a bad fellow and comes from a well-to-do family, he isn't right for my sister. He isn't worthy of her. In one word: It is impossible that I give her to Mihran."

Yacoub then turned to me and said, in a commanding voice: "Don't ever encourage him or become attached to him. I'm sure you know that I have to tell him he has my consent but that my mother and sister are opposing me. I will say I am trying to persuade both of you. After all, he is my close friend, and I have a number of business deals with him that I hope to bring off. But you must continue raising obstacles and, so far as possible, put an end to their hopes."

Later, I told my mother, "My brother must think I'm a child. Not only will I not encourage Mihran or become attached to him, I feel nothing but revulsion for him. Since he is my brother's close friend, and I know the kind of life my brother is leading, I'm certain he, too, is leading that sort of life. It would be impossible for me to marry such a young man."

Mihran grew more and more miserable. He started to lose weight, refused to go to work, and couldn't sleep at night. Slowly, a deep suspicion took root in his tormented heart: Efronia's family was refusing him because they were planning for her to marry the youngest Katchadourian brother, Aram. In his agony, Mihran managed to convey a death threat to Aram's brother Yeghia, who had arranged for Yacoub to work in their pharmacy.

Scared out of his wits, Yeghia rushed over to Ovsannah's house one evening. Efronia, who was cleaning up after their evening meal, was alarmed at the sight of him. She writes:

He was quite flustered and blurted out, "You should either give your daughter to these people in marriage or leave town right away. . . . They suspect we have plans to marry her off to my brother Aram. I have received a written threat—they are going to shoot me if we don't give up this prospect. We have no intention for Aram to marry anyone right now, but I warn you, these people are capable of anything. Please take pity on me. I have a family to worry about . . ."

Meanwhile, my brother was lighting the lamp, and some kerosene spilled on the rug and caught fire. We had a lot of trouble putting it out. Finally, we got Yeghia Effendi to sit down and poured him a glass of brandy. My brother promised he would meet with Mihran and his family and assure them that the Katchadourians had no part in this matter. After a while, my brother took Yeghia home. He was a weak man, and his whole body was still shaking.

But Mihran didn't give up. On the contrary, he redoubled his efforts to see me and convince me of his love. He gave me presents, he wrote letters, he used intermediaries, but the only feeling he could awaken in me was pity.

I really felt sorry for him, because he had taken on the appearance of a madman. I was wishing he would gradually give up hope. But on the contrary, his love for me became even more fierce with time. Seeing his condition, I tried to see if I could awaken some love in my heart for him. But it was useless. My heart had turned to stone as far as he was concerned.

My life in Iskenderun now became unbearable. On one side was Mihran's family, trying to pressure me to change my mind. On the other was my brother's intolerable way of life. There was no solution other than to return to Aintab.

My mother and I began to get ready. Our plan was to leave even before my teaching duties were over, and without letting anyone know. At the very last moment, when all our things were packed and we were ready to set out, we would tell Yacoub.

But after my mother and I had agreed on this plan, certain unforeseen circumstances arose so that I could not stand firm in our decision. I had to tell my mother I had given up the idea of returning to Aintab.

My mother was perplexed. What possible reason could there be for me to want to remain in this place, to have changed my mind so suddenly? All sorts of suspicions entered her mind. She spoke to me sweetly, she spoke to me harshly, but to no avail—she couldn't get an answer out of me.

Finally, I began to cry. I said I had a headache and went to bed. My mother brought me food and coffee. I didn't want to eat. She caressed my face and stroked my hair, asked me to confess my sorrows, and reminded me that she was my mother.

There was nothing Ovsannah could do, however. Thoroughly mystified, she started unpacking the things they had packed for their journey to Aintab.

Only seventy years later, sitting at her small writing desk in California, did Efronia give a full accounting of her refusal to leave Iskenderun that spring.

Part II

RAMZI

The Suitor from Across the Chasm

Up to this point in her manuscript, Efronia's beautiful handwriting flows evenly through close to one hundred pages. Not one word is scratched over; nothing is added between the lines; not a word is misspelled. Writing in her small California apartment, thousands of miles away from where she grew up, Efronia looked at all the turbulence of her young life and described it to us unflinchingly; those years before she turned eighteen must have seemed to her like another life.

But then, something happens. Her writing becomes strained. Some words are crossed out. She forgets a detail, then adds it in the margin.

She writes in a state of emotional turmoil. And then, she writes a heading and underlines it. It says:

The First and Last Time in My Life That I Was in Love.
This is now where I have reached: the life I lived in Iskenderun and the adventures of love I passed through in 1913. But all of a sudden, my unimaginable yet real experience of falling in love appears in my mind's eye like a caravan of camels. I remember. I am shaken, yet I want to write it down. I have thought about it for days: should I write it or should I not, should I remember or should I not?

I don't know how many times I have begun to write but then set it aside.

"I gave it up," I tell myself. "It is a love that was lost and unfulfilled; it's better not to write, not to remember. I have kept it secret so far; let it go to the grave with me."

Finally, I decide to write it down. Even though I lost my love during my life, I will at least remember it in the story of my life and write it down so that his memory will remain alive. I remember a poet who wrote, "When I die, and grass grows on my grave, I am still alive. But should the memory of me die, should I be forgotten, then I shall truly be dead."

My pen is weak in my eighty-eighth year; so many days have passed, so many months and years. How can I remember, how can I describe my undying and unforgettable love and all the emotions I felt in my eighteenth year; how can I write about my sweet dreams just as they were?

Finally, however, she begins:

My brother had rented a house on a good street. A few of our neighbors were Christian Arabs. We almost never visited them. First of all, we did not know Arabic. Also, they had some young men who had approached us with marriage proposals. Needless to say, we refused them all. We just greeted them to be polite.

A few doors down from us, there lived a couple whom we often came across, a respectable and gracious young husband and wife. They were Turks, from Constantinople, and the woman did not cover her face with a veil. Gradually, we became acquainted. One day, I asked my brother if he knew this family. He said, "Yes, I know them well. They are customers of mine. The man is a high-level government official. They are decent people, and it would be fine to see them socially."

One day, I met the wife in the street. She expressed the wish to pay us a visit with her husband. We welcomed them gladly. They came

*over one evening, and my brother introduced them to us: "Shakib Bey
and his wife, Nouriyeh Hanem."*

*We had a good time. We spoke Turkish. My mother was quite
pleased. When they were leaving, my brother thanked them for their
visit and asked the wife if she would treat me as a sister. "My
sister," he said, "feels very lonely. She has almost no friends here."*

*Nouriyeh Hanem turned to my brother and said, "It would be a
great pleasure to get to know your sister; I will love her like my own
true sister."*

*The next time I saw Nouriyeh Hanem, she said, "There is a club
here, and my husband and I are members. We can invite our friends
there. One day, I would like to take you there. Would you like to
come?"*

*I was happy to accept. We set a time for the next day and went to
the club with a few of her friends. I was glad to know them, and I
was glad I had found such a good companion in Nouriyeh Hanem. I
had been bored at home, and I did not like the atmosphere in the
Armenian community; knowing her would give me a pleasant way to
pass my time, and it brought some change into my life.*

*A week later, Nouriyeh Hanem invited me to the club for dinner.
"My husband," she said, "has to go to Antioch in connection with
his work and will not be able to accompany us." I got my mother's
consent, put on a very beautiful dress that had been made for me
recently, and walked to the club. We were seated at a nice table,
where we chatted for a while. Then we had our dinner. Just as we
were having coffee, a young man approached us, greeted us, and,
turning to Nouriyeh Hanem, asked if he could share our table.*

*Nouriyeh Hanem smiled, looked at me, and said, "You are
welcome." She introduced us to each other: "Miss Efronia Nazarian,
the sister of pharmacist Yacoub Nazarian, recently arrived from
Aintab."*

She then turned to me and said: "Ramzi Bey, the son of relatives of mine from Persia."

We shook hands. Nouriyeh Hanem asked him if he had had dinner. He said he had eaten, and we all ordered ice cream for dessert.

During this time he never turned his eyes away from me. His face seemed somehow familiar, but I could not remember where I had seen him. We sat for a while, and then I said, "I would like to stay longer, but I'm afraid I have to go. I should not be late getting home."

To tell the truth, I did not really want to leave, because up to that point in my life—and I can even say up until now in my life—I had never met such a noble, perfectly handsome, gracious young man. His sweet looks, his mellow words—he was the sort of man I had been dreaming of marrying for years. I can't deny it, I can't lie: I fell in love with Ramzi at that very moment. My heart, which had been so hardened toward the many young men who had expressed their love for me, who were mad about me, now softened even before I had heard one single word of love from his lips—and without knowing whether he in turn loved me or not.

We got up. Ramzi came along with me and Nouriyeh Hanem as we were walking home, and when we reached Nouriyeh Hanem's house, he asked, "May I accompany the young lady to her house?" She looked at me. I smiled and said, "I will be grateful." Thanking Nouriyeh Hanem and wishing her good night, Ramzi and I started walking toward my house.

When we got there, he held my hand and asked, "Please forgive me, but may I have a word with you?" I looked at him and smiled. He felt emboldened. He turned to me and said:

"I feel very fortunate today. For months, I have been wishing to see you close up, at least for a few moments, and to speak to you for a few minutes. I owe our meeting to Nouriyeh Hanem, and I am grateful to her for it. My dear, don't think that I saw you only today

and came to love you only today; it's been many months that I have known you and fallen in love with you. No doubt, you saw me for the first time today, but I have known you for a long time. I have seen you every day, but, unlike the other men who have been after you, I haven't pursued you. I haven't crossed your path. I haven't lingered around your house. But every day I hide and wait for you along the streets where you pass. I see you, and I admire your lovely, angelic face. I am tormented day and night by my love and longing for you. Finally, I could be patient no longer; I could stand it no longer. I did not want to express my love and admiration for you through letters. I did not want to stop you on the street and open my heart to you. I searched for someone I could trust, someone to whom I could reveal my secret. I needed someone who would understand a young man in love, who would help me find a way to meet you.

"I found Nouriyeh Hanem. She is a very close friend of our family—she is decent, kind, and trustworthy—and I opened my heart to her. I begged her to help me, to create opportunities for me to see you. As I mentioned, it is to her that I owe our meeting. I shall not say any more today. You must only know I love you, with a sincere and virtuous love. I am in love with you. Be certain that in order to be loved by you in return and to be united with you, I am willing even to sacrifice my life.

"But I do not want to take any more of your time. Good night." With that, he kissed my hand and waited outside until I opened the door and closed it behind me.

When I got in, my mother was still awake. She asked what time it was. I lied and said it was half past nine, when in fact it was past midnight. My mother asked some questions. "Forgive me, mother," I said. "I feel very sleepy, and I have a headache. I will tell you about it tomorrow. Let me just say I had a very good time."

I withdrew into my room and got into bed. But where was my sleep? Where was my rest? I sat up and pressed my hands against my temples. I was in turmoil. My mind was no longer in my head.

I could not forget his eyes, his handsome face. I kept hearing his sweet voice, his gentle words, and his confessions of love during our parting moments.

I tried to pull myself together and think. I asked myself over and over how I could have fallen in love at first glance. I blamed myself: how could this possibly have happened? Then I decided that falling in love is not a sin for a young woman—especially falling in love with a young man like Ramzi.

But how, I asked myself, could our love ever be fulfilled? How could the two of us ever get married—Ramzi, a Persian Moslem, and I, a Christian Armenian girl? I must use my head, I told myself. I must try not to take a wrong step before this love has put down roots.

Although I thought about all of this, I felt as if I were not seeing my situation clearly. I remained silent for a while, and then I lifted my eyes and I prayed:

"My Almighty and loving Lord, my Father, why did you plunge me into this? Why did you awaken this love, for which there is no remedy, in my heart? Why did you place this young man in my path? I beg of you: Just as you filled my heart with love for him, please remove it now. Although I love him, there is an impassable bridge across the chasm that divides us. I beg you to remove this cup from me. I am a weak creature. I beg you, and with my tears I implore you. And if that is going to be impossible, help me at least by showing me a way."

When I finished this prayer, I fell asleep, exhausted.

The next morning, my mother came into my room and woke me for school. She immediately saw that I was not well. She brought me a cup of coffee and asked, "My daughter, what is wrong? Did you perhaps drink something last night that you're not used to?"

I didn't answer. I turned away and said I was not going to go to school that day. I stayed in bed a few hours with a fierce headache. For the rest of that day I stayed indoors with my mother and grandmother.

The following day, I passed by the missionary school that Ramzi attended. He was standing outside. We greeted each other and smiled, and I continued on my way. He did not try to get close to me or to follow me. The delicacy with which he treated me made me feel even more attached to him.

A few days later, Nouriyeh Hanem passed by our house. With my mother's consent, she took me to her house for dinner. Shakib Bey had already eaten; he excused himself and soon left the house.

Not long after, Ramzi arrived. He greeted us joyfully, kissing our hands. It seemed to me that he had become even more handsome. Although she and I had already had our coffee, Nouriyeh Hanem poured more, and we spent a few happy hours together.

As on our previous meeting, Ramzi accompanied me home, but this time we stepped into a side street. He held my hand and said, "The happiest hours of my life have been the hours I have spent with you." Once again, he asked if he could speak with me for a few minutes.

What could I say? It was dark, and we were hiding. He whispered, "Our meeting this evening has given me hope and life. I pray to God that He fulfills our sincere love for each other and that He unites us until death. My darling, the flame of your love scorches my heart. I cannot live this life without you, be certain of that. I beg you that we not keep this love a secret anymore. Let us tell our parents, obtain their consent, and get married."

He talked and talked, but I remained silent. Finally, he asked, "My dear, why don't you say something? Do you love me? Do you accept my proposal? Speak up and put out this fire burning in my heart."

I waited. For one moment, I considered making it clear to him how impossible it was that we would ever get married. But love is blind. I could not bring myself to do it. Finally, I turned to him.

59

"Ramzi, my dear, just as you love me, I must confess that I have also fallen in love with you. I have loved you from the first moment I saw you. I want you to know that your wishes are mine, too. But let us not rush and tell our parents yet. I am afraid we may not get their consent and then they will forbid us to see each other. So let's not rush things. There are many obstacles to our union. You still have your education to finish, and you need to get yourself established. You're not old enough yet to get married."

He would not let me finish. "None of the things you're telling me are obstacles to our getting married. I could be married and still continue my education. I don't need money. My family doesn't need me to help them. I beg you to spare me this torment. Give me your consent and put me at ease."

I turned to him and said, "I beg you, don't go any further. Give me some time to reach a decision. Let us for now find occasions to meet and enjoy each other's company. And let us leave the rest to God to arrange as He sees fit."

Ramzi interrupted me again and said, "There is fear in my heart. I hear that you have many suitors. Do you promise that you will not marry one of them?"

"I swear to God with all my heart I will not marry any one of them," I said. "I will never exchange your love for the love of anyone else."

He kissed me, and we parted.

I entered my house fearfully. My mother was still awake.

"My dear, you're late," she said. "I was afraid your brother would get here before you and ask where you were."

We sat and talked for a while, and then I went to bed. I felt exhausted and overwhelmed. I wished that I didn't have this awful secret and that I could summon the strength to reach a decision one way or the other.

Efronia knew very well what she was up against. Ramzi was indeed on the other side of a chasm. He shared his religion with the man who had murdered Efronia's father. If she married him, she was certain to be cast out not only from her family but from the whole community that had been her life until that time.

How could she bring herself to tell him this?

A Terrible Dilemma

By this time, it was late spring. At the school where Efronia taught, there was a lot to do: meetings to attend, final exams to prepare, graduation ceremonies to rehearse. Efronia worked hard, but her heart was not in it. Increasingly, she felt torn between her growing love for Ramzi and her growing conviction that their marriage was impossible.

To buy time, she blamed her busy schedule and avoided meeting Ramzi and Nouriyeh Hanem. This made the situation even worse. She could see how Ramzi suffered and how puzzled Nouriyeh Hanem was over her behavior.

Very soon, she told herself, she would have to tell Ramzi that the dream was over. But he had his own ideas. She writes:

One morning, on my way to school, Ramzi passed me and handed me an envelope. I took it and continued on my way. The envelope contained an invitation to dinner at the club with Nouriyeh Hanem.

She and I got to the club the next day at six. Ramzi was already there and had ordered a table set up in a private room. He thanked us for accepting his invitation and soon we were having dinner. We had a very good time. Ramzi told us about his final exams and invited us to his graduation ceremony. He told us he had been accepted at a university in London to pursue his higher education.

Without thinking, I asked him what field he would pursue.

"I have one year to decide," he said. "But let me ask you, what field would you prefer that I pursue?"

I was very sorry I had asked that question. I said: "The choice belongs to you. What field do you feel attracted to?"

"There are two choices," he said. "One is the law, and the other is the military. There is still time to decide."

When it finally was time to go, we again accompanied Nouriyeh Hanem to her house and then started walking toward mine. When we came close, we saw that the light was on in my brother's room. We quickly said goodnight, Ramzi kissed me, and we parted.

I opened the door slowly. My brother was awake, and when he heard me come in, he came down from his room.

"Are you coming from Nouriyeh Hanem's?" he asked.

"Yes," I said. "I was invited to dinner with one of her woman friends."

"This friendship with Nouriyeh Hanem has turned out very well for you," he said.

"Yes, my brother. God Himself must have arranged it for me."

The next day on my way to work I passed by Ramzi's school again. I saw him standing in front of the gate. He gave me a letter. I could not read the letter in school, so I went home for lunch. I withdrew to my room, and when I read the letter, I could not restrain my tears.

So many years have passed. It is impossible to remember everything in that letter. I know only that there were no words of love in the dictionary that Ramzi had not used. Poor boy. The letter was full of hopes for the future, sweet dreams, pleadings, yearnings, and fantasies. He hoped we would get engaged and married shortly; he begged to see me soon.

When I read that letter, my heart sank. If his marriage proposal had had any likelihood of fulfillment, I would have considered myself the most fortunate girl in the world. He was a very handsome boy, endowed with the best attributes, and the son of a rich family. He loved me sincerely and to the point of madness, and I loved him in return. I wanted to marry him with all my heart. Where would I find another young man like him?

But a chasm lay between us that was impossible to cross. A storm raged in my mind. I could not sleep at night or rest during the day. I knew it was not right for us to continue our relationship. If we continued to see each other, I knew our love would only grow deeper and bring about bad consequences.

After days of torment, I decided to turn to Nouriyeh Hanem. But how would I reveal the obstacle that stood in the way of my marrying Ramzi? She herself was a Moslem. Would she not feel bad? Would she not take offense? Would she not feel hurt?

In the midst of these worries, I fell ill and went to bed with a very high fever. The doctor said I had malaria. He gave me some drugs. I felt as if I was on fire, and I stayed in bed for several days.

Nouriyeh Hanem had become worried about me, and one day she stopped by the house to see me. My mother offered her coffee and thanked her for her visit, but I could not get out of bed to see her. I felt very tired and I had a terrible headache. My mother became very worried. My brother would come home for both lunch and dinner during those days. He slept at home more frequently, too, and took more of an interest in me.

A few days later, Nouriyeh Hanem returned with a lovely bouquet of flowers. My mother was out shopping. We placed the flowers in a vase on my table. She took out a card and showed it to me—the flowers were from Ramzi. Reading the card, I could not restrain my tears. Even though there were only a few lines, they said things that tore my heart to pieces. Ramzi wondered if he had hurt my feelings with a wrong word or expression and pleaded that I put his fears to rest with a few lines. I felt obliged to answer him. I wrote, "My dear, have no doubts. Just as you are tormented by your love for me, so am I by my love for you. Let us pray to God for help."

Chapter 9

Nouriyeh Hanem looked at me and said: "My dear sister, it is now necessary that we open our hearts to each other. I understand you as I understand Ramzi, and I know the condition he is in. However, I promised Ramzi that before you and I have a serious talk, the two of you should meet some evening, at our house or at the club."

I could not refuse. A few days later, I was well enough to go to school. On my way, I passed the school and saw Ramzi waiting outside for me. Approaching me, he expressed his joy at seeing me well and thanked me for responding to his note. He wanted to see me as soon as possible.

A few days later, still feeling a little weak, I went to the club with Nouriyeh Hanem. Within a quarter of an hour Ramzi came. He looked happy. We sat for a while until it was time for dinner. He very much wanted us to be his guests, and we were glad to accept.

That evening, they were playing some lovely music at the club. Although the place was crowded, I knew no one there, since this was mainly a club for Moslems. Ramzi danced with Nouriyeh Hanem, and then he proposed that I dance with him. I demurred, saying that I did not know how to dance well, but I finally gave in. When I got up, my legs were trembling. We danced a few times; he was a very good dancer.

We had a wonderful time, and toward the end of the evening, he told me and Nouriyeh Hanem that the following day was his parents' twenty-fifth anniversary. There was going to be a big party at his house, and he invited me to come along with Nouriyeh Hanem and Shakib Bey. I thanked him, and, as was customary, wished long life to his parents.

We got up and, as usual, walked Nouriyeh Hanem to her house. Then, he escorted me home, and we again went around to the back of the house and talked for a while.

"I very much hope we will celebrate the twenty-fifth and the fiftieth anniversary of our wedding," he said, adding that he hoped I would come to the celebration the next day as the guest of Nouriyeh Hanem.

66

"I thank you, but I cannot come," I said.

"When will the day come when we can see each other freely?" he asked.

We kissed and parted.

Several days passed. I saw Nouriyeh Hanem and knew the time had come to keep my word and reveal to her my problem with Ramzi. We agreed to meet the following morning at her house. I sent word to the school that I was not feeling well and went over to Nouriyeh Hanem's with a heavy heart.

Efronia's Confession

Nouriyeh Hanem sat down next to me and said: "My dear, just as Ramzi opened his heart to me, you too must now confess to me without holding anything back. And just as I promised Ramzi, I also promise you to do everything possible to help you and to share the burden of your difficulties.

"I realize that you feel bewildered. I can see that you are buried in thought. Yet I can make no sense of your condition. I understood from Ramzi that you are in a state of uncertainty. Whatever he proposes, you do not consent. You keep finding obstacles; you say it is not the right time. All this torments him greatly.

"I think I have told you this already: While you have known him only for a few months, he has known you much longer. He told me where he first saw you, how he found out who you were, and how he fell in love with you.

"Ramzi did not have the courage to tell his parents about you, and he was tormented for many days. Whom could he confide in? Who could help him? Then he learned that I knew you and that we saw each other, and he came to me. My husband and I have been intimate friends of his family for a long time; they love me as they love their own sister. 'Please help me,' he said. 'I have no one to talk to. I have come to you for help; please listen to me.'

"I asked him how I could help him, and he began to tell me how he had seen you and fallen in love with you. Seeing the state he was

in, I said, "Ramzi my dear, don't worry and don't torment yourself.
I will do everything I can to fulfill your wishes.

"There is no need to say more. I promised him I would introduce
you to each other and create opportunities for you to meet. There is no
need to repeat what has happened since then—you yourself are well
aware of it. Let me just tell you that had I not known Ramzi and
trusted him, I would never have made that promise.

"Look, my dear sister," she said to me, "just as I love him, I have
also come to love you. I thought it was a good thing to make young
people like you two happy and to help them get married. I haven't
changed my mind. My dear, this is a great opportunity for you. I
cannot praise Ramzi enough. Such a young man, in this day and
age, is very rare. He is kind, the son of a noble family, very rich,
very handsome, and most gracious. His father is only a consul here,
but in Persia he is an eminent man. Since you have been seeing Ramzi
for some time now, you know what a decent and highly moral man
he is.

"There is no need to say more about him. I have also come to know
and love you. Like Ramzi, you are a gracious person endowed with
the best qualities. You deserve each other. I am certain that when his
parents get to know you and hear about Ramzi's proposal to you, they
will give their consent right away. Because he is their most beloved
son, they will make every necessary sacrifice.

"Dear sister, don't you think I know about the immoral fellows
pursuing you? You can be sure their only aim is to lay their hands on
a girl like you. Please talk to me candidly. Open your heart to me,
and reveal your thoughts. As I said, and I mean it most sincerely, I
will do everything in my power to help you. Please do not keep
anything from me. Why don't you agree to any of his proposals? Why
do you not satisfy his yearnings? What are you waiting for, and
why are you tormenting him? Please, open your heart to me, and tell
me what obstacles are stopping you from marrying him."

I looked at her and couldn't hold my tears back. I said, "My dear sister, everything you say is true. I understand very well. You are concerned about our welfare and happiness. You have done everything you could. I do appreciate it and I feel grateful to you. Never in all my life will I forget what you have done."

"Yes, I will open my heart to you. I have wanted to tell you everything and ask you to help, but I have not had the courage. My dear sister, when I first saw Ramzi, I fell in love with him. Just as Ramzi loves me, I, too, love and worship him. I have never in my life met such a gracious young man. I am sure I will never find such a man again. I have always dreamed of marrying someone like him.

"When he walked home from the club with me that first evening and wanted to say a few words, I gladly agreed. And then he opened his heart to me and confessed the love he had felt for me over the past months. He expressed his wish to marry me.

"After I left him, I went to my room and sat down on my bed. Instead of feeling happy, I was tormented for hours; a storm was raging in my mind. I cannot tell you how I suffered. I could not get his image out of my mind for a single moment. I wished I had never met him. I implored God to take this love out of my heart."

Nouriyeh Hanem cut me short: "But why did you have these thoughts? Tell me, confess to me."

I said, "How can I confess? How can I speak, when my tongue refuses to obey me? If I confess, will you feel hurt? Will you be offended?"

Tears were streaming down my face. I could not continue. Nouriyeh Hanem came close to me, wiped my tears, caressed my face, and brought me some water to drink. "Efronia, I promise I won't be upset, whatever you say," she told me.

I stopped crying and took a deep breath. Then I hugged her and said, "My mind feels numb. If it's not too much trouble, may we have some coffee so that I can collect my thoughts?"

After I had my first sip of coffee, I continued: "Dear sister, let me first beg your forgiveness. I am guilty. I must confess that when you *introduced me to him, you told me who he was. When he took me home and confessed his love for me and expressed his desire to marry me—at that very moment I should have told him it was impossible for me to marry him.*

"But the moment I saw him, I fell in love with him. I could not think straight. I could not speak up. Love is blind. So, despite my problem, we began to see each other. We became attached. Yet for all this time now, a problem has been tormenting me. I feel guilty for never having spoken about it, but now, no matter how difficult it is, I have to do it.

"Dear sister, I cannot marry Ramzi. Ramzi is a Persian Moslem and I am an Armenian Christian girl. There is a deep chasm between us. How can we join each other in marriage? As I said, I should not have entered this relationship, knowing how impossible it was. How will Ramzi ever forgive me? How will you ever forgive me? I am certain God himself will never forgive me. Dear sister, what else can I say but to beg you to help me and to show me a way out of this."

Nouriyeh Hanem turned to me and said: "Calm down, dear sister. If this is the only problem, your situation is not hopeless. Several of Ramzi's relatives have married Europeans. His own grandmother is French. You, too, will be one of them. The Persians and the Armenians are very close to each other, and members of his family especially are like Europeans. All their children go to foreign schools. Ramzi himself first attended a Jesuit school, and now he is studying at the Protestant mission school. They are very liberal-minded."

I interrupted her. "Dear sister, as I have said so many times, I do not want to hurt your feelings or insult you. Ramzi's being Moslem is not a stain on his character. Every man's nation and religion is holy to him. Far be it from me to blame him for that. But I must confess that we Armenians are not like Europeans—our situation is different.

"The issue is not just one of religion. Under the Turkish govern-ment, Armenians have been persecuted, tortured, slaughtered, and

*plundered for a long time. I am sorry to say that I myself am a child
of an Armenian martyr. During the Turkish massacres in Aintab,
my father was murdered. My mother was left alone with five children
when I was two months old.*

"*How can I remove this obstacle, even for the sake of Ramzi's love
for me, and mine for him? Tell me, how can I marry Ramzi, when
my family and my nation have such strong feelings against the Turks?
Would my family ever forgive me? What would other Armenians
think? As I said to you, I wish I had never seen him, I wish I did
not love him. Surely by rejecting his sincere and pure love, I am going
to be unhappy for the rest of my life. And I am greatly troubled by
the unhappiness I will cause him. I am guilty, and I beg your
forgiveness, and his, with my tears. I am responsible for all that has
happened. May God, too, forgive me. May He not count it a sin.
Love made me helpless. Here, then, dear sister, is my sorrow, my
secret, and my guilt. I beg you to help me and show me a way out.*"

*Nouriyeh Hanem was silent for a few minutes. Then she said,
"My dear, I, too, find myself in a very difficult situation. Although
the obstacle you have revealed does not seem insurmountable to me, I
do understand your problem. And to some extent I agree with you.
But please, do not blame yourself and do not torment yourself.*

"*Yes, although you loved Ramzi from the first moment, since you
saw no possibility of ever marrying him, you should not have entered
this relationship. And you should not have kept Ramzi's hopes alive.
And your own, too. But all that is in the past, and we have to think
about the present. How could we possibly persuade him to give you
up? I can tell you right away that even if you had expressed these
reservations from the very beginning, he would not have been willing
to give you up. And now it is even more impossible, and it is going to
be very painful.*

"*I have seen many others in love, and I, too, married my husband
after I fell in love with him. But had circumstances been unsuitable,
we could have given each other up. I have never seen anyone worship*

73

someone the way Ramzi worships you, however. How will we ever prevail on him to give up the idea of marrying you? It is a settled matter for him. He is thinking of asking his parents' consent, so that you can get engaged.

"And he wants to marry you before he goes to London.

"Look, my sister, it will be hard for us to think about this any further or reach any decision now. And it would not be right, because I can see and understand the state you are in. If you like, let's each think about this some more. As of today, are you going to be able to give him up? Everything is possible in life. Your decision is going to affect him a great deal."

I was unable to respond to her, and I remained silent. Then Nouriyeh Hanem said, "Let us not hurry. Let us not take a wrong step. Until we reach a definite decision, let your relationship continue."

"Yes," I said.

"I promised Ramzi I would create an opportunity for you to get together soon. He is waiting impatiently for some news from you."

I said, "Saturday would be convenient for me. My brother is going to Antioch."

I returned home. It was noon. My mother thought I had just come from school. She had already set the lunch table. I remember very well that we had squash dolma *that day. My brother came and sat down with us. I had no appetite and had to force myself to eat.*

After lunch, I excused myself, took an aspirin, and went to bed.

Someone Else Gets Involved

At five o'clock on Saturday afternoon, Nouriyeh Hanem and I met at the club. We had agreed to meet a little early, so that we would have a chance to talk before Ramzi arrived. Neither of us could reach a final decision. We thought it would be best to do nothing further until Ramzi's school and my school ended, so that he would not be distracted from his exams and I from my duties. Thus, we decided only that for the next ten to fifteen days, Ramzi and I should not meet each other and should attend to our responsibilities with calm minds. In that way, we would also gain some time to reach a decision.

Ramzi came a bit late but appeared very happy. He spoke about his forthcoming exams and again invited us to his graduation ceremony. He ordered drinks and food for us. We ate and drank. When we got up to leave, Ramzi turned to me and Nouriyeh Hanem and said, "I hope we shall see each other again soon."

"Ramzi, for the next ten to fifteen days both you and Efronia are busy. Let us postpone our next meeting for a while. But then, when you receive your diploma, I am going to give a party in your honor at our house."

I sensed that Ramzi was not very happy with Nouriyeh Hanem's plan, but he said nothing. As on earlier occasions, we left Nouriyeh Hanem at her house and started walking toward mine. We talked for a while. He expressed his disappointment with Nouriyeh Hanem's plan, and then he said: "For several days now, my mother has been suspicious. I don't know why, but she keeps questioning me and telling me that she and my father would consent to my getting married before I go to London. She says that although I am not quite of an age to marry, she is concerned that I may fall for an unsuitable girl in London. She says there are many good girls around here and that she and my father will get for me whomever I choose.

"I laughed and told her not to be afraid; I would not easily fall for those temptations. But then I wondered if I should perhaps tell her about my having fallen in love with you, introduce you to each other, and reveal my wish to marry you. But I did not want to do this without your consent.

"Look, my dear Efronia, this is important. I must inform my parents. We should not let any more time pass."

"We still have time," I said. "The next ten to fifteen days will pass quickly. Just as Nouriyeh Hanem said, both you and I are busy now, and we should not preoccupy our minds with this issue."

Ramzi reluctantly agreed. But he asked me to be sure to pass by his school during these next two weeks, so that we would at least see each other. We said good night and parted.

Five or six days later, Nouriyeh Hanem's maid, Ayisheh, came to our house and said, "My lady sent me to call you over for a few moments."

I was perplexed. What could have happened? I dressed and went over immediately. Nouriyeh Hanem met me at the door and escorted me to the living room, where a lady was sitting. She was a beautiful woman of medium height and rather plump. She got up, and Nouriyeh Hanem introduced me to her as "Efronia Nazarian, the sister of pharmacist Yacoub Effendi" and her to me as "the wife of Nematollah, Farouz Hanem." The woman looked at my face and said, "May God keep you. Blessed be Allah, what wonders He creates."

We sat and talked. She asked me quite a few questions, such as where I was from and when I had arrived. When she asked about my family, I said I had a mother, two brothers, and two sisters. She asked about my father then, and I told her he had been killed when I was two months old, in 1895, during the massacre of the Armenians by the Turks in Aintab.

Hearing this, she changed the subject quickly and asked me some other questions, all of which I answered.

Nouriyeh Hanem brought some tea—the Persians like tea very much. I stayed a while longer and then excused myself and returned home. Although Nouriyeh Hanem had not said that the woman was Ramzi's mother, I knew that's who she was. I also knew the two families were intimate friends and that they often visited each other, but I could not understand why Nouriyeh Hanem had wanted to introduce me to her.

The next day, as I was passing by Nouriyeh Hanem's house, she saw me and called me in.

"The woman you met yesterday was Ramzi's mother," she said.

"I guessed so," I said. "She is a fine and sweet lady."

"After you left," Nouriyeh Hanem said, "she confided in me and explained why she had come to see me. This is what she told me:

" 'One morning recently, I came into Ramzi's room and saw that his bed had not yet been made. The maids usually arrange his bed every morning, and then I tidy up his room. This time, I did not wait for them and made his bed myself. When I was arranging his bedding, I found the photograph of a young woman. First I thought she was a movie star, but when I looked more closely, I was certain it was the girl I saw at your house today.

" 'The next morning, I noticed Ramzi had taken the photograph away. I thought I would test him and see if he would reveal the identity of the girl. So I said, "My dear son—as I already told you—although you are rather young to get married, you are going to study in London for three years. You are an attractive boy, and many girls will be after you. I fear you may become attached to someone unsuitable. Therefore, if there is a girl here whom you love, let us get

77

you engaged to her or even marry you off to her, so that you can go together to London."

" 'I noticed that Ramzi's face brightened up. "Is it true, Mother," he asked me, "that if I want to get married, you will consent to it?"

" ' "Most gladly, my son," I told him.

" 'He then took out of his pocket the same photograph I had found under his pillow and said, "Mother, if you can arrange for me to marry this girl, I won't hesitate for one moment to marry her."

" 'I asked him if he knew her well, whether she was worthy of him, and if she came from a good family. "Yes, Mother," he said, "you can trust me. I saw her five or six months ago and fell in love with her. I did not have the courage to tell you. I did not know where to turn and how to get to know her. I thought Nouriyeh Hanem could help me, since they are neighbors and know each other. Mother, please, do not ask me to tell you anything more. Instead, go to Nouriyeh Hanem, who knows all about my relationship with this girl. You can learn everything directly from her."

" 'And that is how I came to see you, my dear. I have not told my husband anything yet because I wanted to get some information from you first.' "*

"Efronia, let me tell you more about my conversation with Ramzi's mother," said Nouriyeh Hanem. "First of all, I told her she had done the right thing by coming to see me. I said I felt an obligation to explain matters and to tell her things I had not been able to tell her. I asked for her forgiveness for not having done so earlier, and I promised to tell her everything I knew.

"I then proceeded to relate to her, in great detail, everything that had gone on from the very first day that Ramzi came to see me: how he had asked to be introduced to you, how the two of you had fallen in love with each other, and how I had continued to arrange for you to meet.

"I also told her about the last conversation you and I had. When

I finished telling her about your problem, Farouz Hanem fell silent and looked confused. She told me, 'My sister, I find myself in a very difficult situation. If this girl finds it impossible to marry my son, why did she not say so from the very beginning? Instead, she has carried on this relationship with Ramzi, and continues to do so now.

" 'Ramzi has been living with high hopes; they have become attached to each other. How are they now going to part? And if she leaves him, what will become of my poor son?' "

"I told Farouz Hanem she was right in everything she said and that I wished you had at least told me about this problem right from the beginning, not months later. But I also told her not to blame you, but to know you loved Ramzi very much. You are young and inexperienced, I said, and you just didn't have the courage to tell Ramzi. And I told her about all your tears when you admitted your fault to me, and how troubled your conscience was.

"Farouz Hanem was silent for a long time. Then she said, 'My sister, when my son learns about this problem, what sort of a state is he going to fall into?' I told her God was great and that there was still time. I also asked her not to tell Ramzi she had met you or that she had talked to me.

"When Farouz Hanem left my house, she looked depressed and said she hoped we would meet again soon to talk some more."

I listened to Nouriyeh Hanem's words. I still could not give her a definitive answer. I just thanked her and went home. Now there was a fourth person involved. I wondered what Ramzi's mother would do, if anything. I felt torn by my thoughts, and at times I found myself in such a state that I felt ready to tell my mother everything, regardless of the consequences. Then, I thought, she and I would quietly arrange to go back to Aintab, without letting anyone know. But, then again, I did not see how I could possibly abandon Ramzi like that.

My will was very weak.

79

The following Sunday, I accompanied my mother to church. The assembly hall of Ramzi's school was used on Sundays for the Protestant church services. After the service, the headmistress of the school approached us and gave us two tickets for the graduation ceremonies of their school the following Sunday. This made me very happy. Although Ramzi had invited me, I could not have accepted his invitation. Now that the school had invited us, it was possible for me to attend.

On Sunday, my mother and I went to the graduation. I saw Nouriyeh Hanem sitting next to Ramzi's parents in the first row. A while later, the graduates filed in: eight girls and four boys, and one of the boys was Ramzi. He looked radiant and handsome in his graduation uniform.

It was a very well organized ceremony. Each of the graduates read a composition. Ramzi was last, and his composition was the valedictory address. It was greeted with much applause. At the end of the ceremony, my mother and I went up to congratulate the graduates. Nouriyeh Hanem approached us and introduced us to Ramzi's parents. We congratulated them and returned home.

12

Trvandah Buys Some Time

Ramzi's graduation had come and gone, and Efronia's school was over for the summer. But instead of seeing her problem more clearly, Efronia felt as if her mind was in a fog, just like the humid summer air that now enveloped Iskenderun. No matter how much she thought about it, she could see no solution: She could either choose Ramzi and risk complete alienation from her family, or choose her family and her community. There was no middle ground, no possible compromise. Whichever way she turned, she was going to hurt someone she loved.

Nouriyeh Hanem did not make things easier. Instead of holding off and allowing Efronia time to think, Nouriyeh Hanem created more opportunities for her to be with Ramzi. One day, she again sent her maid over to ask if she and her husband could come for a visit in the evening. That was nothing unusual, and Ovsannah gladly bade them welcome. The two families spent a happy evening together; Yacoub, for once, was at home and in a good mood. Before Nouriyeh Hanem and her husband left, they made a counter-invitation: Could Ovsannah and her family come to their house for dinner the next evening?

There were the usual protests about not wanting to cause trouble, but finally Ovsannah and Yacoub accepted. Shakib

Bey, Nouriyeh Hanem's husband, then wondered if his guests would object if the family of Nematollah Bey joined them.

"Not in the least," answered Yacoub. "On the contrary, I would be honored by their presence. I have great respect for that man."

Efronia bolted up to her room. What had gotten into Nouriyeh Hanem? Why was she now inviting Ramzi's family to meet hers, when they had agreed to do precisely the opposite: stay away from each other for a while.

But it was too late to do anything. The next evening at seven o'clock, Efronia's family walked to Nouriyeh Hanem's with a big bouquet of flowers. Ramzi's family had already arrived. Introductions were made, and drinks were served, and after a while they all sat down to a lavish table.

"Everyone was happy," writes Efronia. Then she adds: "Although I, too, tried to be happy, my heart was bleeding."

When they got home that evening, Yacoub was in a good mood.

"What gracious people," Efronia remembers him saying. "It is well worth knowing them. And how graceful and polite their children are. Especially that oldest boy, Ramzi. He used to come to the pharmacy once in a while, but now they send the younger brother. What a handsome and presentable young man Ramzi has become."

This was the moment Ovsannah had been waiting for. The contrast between Ramzi's family and her own son's reputation in town had been weighing heavily on her all evening, and she could no longer contain herself. She lit into Yacoub:

"Now you wish to keep company with families like these. Where have you been for the past nine months since you brought us here and closeted us in this house? If you had taken any interest in us, you, too, would have enjoyed our

82

company, and the company of people like these. Let me tell you, Yacoub, I have regretted a thousand times ever coming to Iskenderun, and I'm counting the days until we leave. Why can't you see the kind of life you are leading? Is it a proper life? And isn't it a pity and an insult to your manhood and to your position that you are in debt up to your neck? The Katchadourians are very unhappy with you, and they are constantly complaining. And to get out from under your debts, you fell as low as using your sister, forcing her to feign affection for Mihran and to give him false hopes. We know very well that that boy leads exactly the same kind of life that you do. He is a low character. I tell you, I am glad my brave daughter finally lost her patience and flatly refused to play along with your games any longer. We have told Mihran's family exactly where things stand, and we have cut off all their hopes.

"And now, even if they have not been after her for a while, my poor girl is afraid to go out—there have been many threats about which you know nothing. You have not cared about any of us. We left your poor brother in Aintab with his sisters. He will be graduating next month. Have you taken any interest in him at all? Do you ever wonder if he needs anything? Do you ever think about him? Are you prepared to make the necessary sacrifices to send him to Beirut next year to study medicine? You know we have spent everything we have on you. We have made every possible sacrifice—and this is the state we find ourselves in, and this is the state that you are in!"

Ovsannah burst into tears. Yacoub stood as if frozen, unable to say a word. Efronia went over to her mother, tried to console her, and took her to her room.

In the wake of this outburst by his mother, Yacoub began

to come home more often, "but to what avail," says Efronia, "since by then our hearts had been broken by him."

After the evening at Nouriyeh Hanem's, Efronia's mood soured even more. She reached a point where she felt ready to give up on everything and leave Iskenderun. Ovsannah and her mother, Trvandah, could not wait to get back to Aintab. The waiting period that Efronia and Nouriyeh Hanem had agreed upon was not yet up, but Efronia was beginning to wonder if she could make her mother stay that long.

The days were now getting unbearably hot and humid. It did not cool off at night; Efronia would toss and turn under the mosquito netting. And in the middle of all this, Grandmother Trvandah became seriously ill.

Her shriveled old body shook with chills in the summer heat; her head was aching, her stomach hurt. On the fourth day, she was delirious. The doctor did not hesitate in his diagnosis: Trvandah had typhoid fever. She was not to be moved; she should not even move about in bed.

Leaving Iskenderun was out of the question for the moment. Efronia wondered if God's hand wasn't somehow in this.

Even though the doctor had told Ovsannah and Efronia that the disease was extremely contagious, Nouriyeh Hanem insisted on visiting, promising to stay at a distance from Trvandah.

Trvandah got progressively worse. The doctor said it would be three weeks before they would know if she was out of danger.

Three weeks! Even under the circumstances, it seemed to Efronia like a gift from God.

One day, Nouriyeh Hanem insisted on taking Efronia out for a change of air, and Ovsannah consented. The next day, Efronia had lunch at Nouriyeh Hanem's house, and late in the afternoon, when it was already getting dark, Nouriyeh Hanem sent her servant to let Ovsannah know that she and Efronia would pay a visit to a friend. Since Yacoub was home, Ovsannah would not be left alone with Trvandah.

After a few minutes, Ramzi appeared at Nouriyeh Hanem's. Overjoyed at seeing Efronia, he suggested that he bring a carriage and take them all to his house.

The ploy was a success; Efronia was taken by surprise. Before she knew it, she was in a carriage, on her way to Ramzi's house. In her memoirs, she describes what happened there:

It was almost dark when we got to their house. We were met at the door, and stepping in, I was amazed at the lovely furnishings; it was as if I had walked into paradise. The entire family was present. Farouz Hanem kissed me and took me to her husband. Although we had met before, she again introduced us. He asked about my mother and my brother and expressed his regrets about my grandmother's illness.

We then went to the dining room. I could not stop admiring the elegance and orderliness of everything. Several maids were standing by, and there were many fine dishes on the table. A samovar was boiling on a side table. I said to myself, "How I wish that today was the day of my wedding to Ramzi. I never want to leave this house and be separated from them." Sweet dreams, but would they ever be fulfilled?

Too soon, this magical evening ended. As her carriage clattered along the corniche and back through narrow streets toward her house, Efronia thought about the contrast between the house she had just seen and what awaited her at home: the old grandmother with typhoid fever; the brother with his sordid life; the mother to whom she couldn't tell her secret.

85

Chapter 12

Seventy years later, she still remembered those as "unbearable days."

But more troubles were to come. One morning, Nouriyeh Hanem dropped by to tell her that Ramzi's mother insisted on a meeting with her, in private.

13

Farouz Hanem to the Rescue

Three days later, on a Saturday morning, Efronia walked over to Nouriyeh Hanem's with trembling legs. Farouz Hanem was waiting for her there. She seemed to know how anxious Efronia was and did her best to put the younger woman at ease. She kissed her and made her sit down nearby, took her hands into hers, and gave her a reassuring smile. Here is how Efronia describes the meeting:

"My very dear girl," said Farouz Hanem, "you are the beloved of my dearest son. I have come here today to open my heart to you as a mother. You, too, like a daughter, must be candid with me.

"I do not wish to go over past events. My dear son and you have become very attached to each other. We, as parents, have no objection to your union. We have come to love you and to think of you as worthy of our son, and we are very happy. We have no reason to want to separate you two or to deprive you of each other. Both Ramzi's father and I want to fulfill the longing of our dear son to marry you. We will rejoice in your happiness.

"But in order to bring this about, you must make a decision. Unless you are indeed going to marry each other, your relationship is meaningless, and it is not right. I want to hear you tell me, just as you have told Nouriyeh Hanem, about the problem you have in marrying Ramzi. We shall do all we can to resolve it.

"I have already spoken with my son. He revealed to me all that is

in his heart, from the very first moment he saw you until today. There is no need to talk at length. He loves you and he worships you. His only wish is to be married to you. But when I saw the intensity of his desire, I must confess I could not bring myself to tell him quite openly about your problem. I simply did not have the courage to kill his hopes. But there is something I want to tell you.

"Look, my dear, what you see as an obstacle has no significance for us whatsoever. We are not like the Turks living with you in Turkey. We are Persian. We are very close to the Armenians, and we have never felt any animosity toward the Armenians at any time. We have always lived with each other in love and peace. My daughter, I would have agreed with you if we were Turks from Aintab. But I am sure that you have no idea who we Persians are. Nouriyeh Hanem has already told you that several European women have married into our family. My husband's mother is French. You will be our Armenian bride.

"My dear, rest assured that by becoming our bride, by marrying Ramzi, you will be most fortunate. And my son will be fortunate, too, marrying an educated, beautiful, and gracious woman like you. My dear, is this really reason enough to deprive yourself of such good fortune? If you and Ramzi separate, I am certain you will both be extremely unhappy.

"My dear, why are you silent? Please, have courage, speak up. Remember that I am your mother, too."

I looked at her face. "Dear Farouz Hanem," I said, "I am most grateful for your kind thoughts for our good fortune, and all your reassurances. I know you are prepared to make every possible sacrifice for our coming together and for our happiness. Let me in turn say that, at this very moment, I am ready to marry Ramzi. If I do not marry him, my world is going to be plunged into darkness. But . . ."

I began to cry. "With my tears I beg your forgiveness. I can hardly look at your face, I feel so ashamed. How will I express myself to

refined people like you, and to my beloved Ramzi, whom I worship?
My tongue refuses to obey me, yet I must confess.

"Differences of nationality and religion are no problem to me, just
as they are no problem to you. We all worship the same God. But here
is my difficulty: Will my family ever consent to my marriage? And
if I get married without their consent, will they ever forgive me? How
will my community look at me? You are a wise woman. Please, help
me, show me a way."

I choked on my tears.

Farouz Hanem embraced me. "Calm down, my dear. Do not cry,"
she said. "I believe Almighty God will help you and that He will
unite innocent lovers like you two. Please trust in God, and trust in
us; we shall find a way out of your difficulties." She dried my tears.
Nouriyeh Hanem served us coffee, and I returned home.

I entered the house feeling very moved but also very upset. I was in
complete turmoil. I could not decide what to do, what to think. My
mind had stopped. My heart was bleeding. Had it been up to me, I
would have made up my mind not on that day but long before. But I
knew that if I married Ramzi, I would not only have my whole
community against me, but my whole family, as well: my mother,
my brothers, my sisters, and all my other relatives. I was in an
impossible situation.

But then I stopped and thought. I tried to imagine our return to
Aintab and what was waiting for me there. Several times, my mother
had told me, "When we return, my cousin's son will have received his
medical diploma. I promised his mother on her deathbed that I would
marry you off to her son. I intend to keep my promise to them, and
you are going to consent to it. He is a fine young man. He is a doctor.
I will marry you off to him. And I will be free at last of all these
problems."

When I thought about these things—about giving up Ramzi,
about marrying someone else, instead, whom I did not love or even

*like—I felt as if I had been struck by lightning. I fell down on my
bed and began to sob. I lifted my eyes to God; I prayed and pleaded.*

*Suddenly, I felt as if some unknown strength had entered me. I
knew I would rather die than give up my beloved, that no matter
what happened and what difficulties I faced, I was going to marry
Ramzi. If necessary, we would wander from country to country; I
could reconcile myself to that. I decided to meet with Ramzi and to
talk it over with him.*

A feeling of lightness came over me.

My grandmother's health improved gradually; after a month she
began to get out of bed and eat light food, but she was still very
weak. My mother asked the doctor if she could travel, but he told her
we would have to wait at least another three weeks or a month. Had
she been able to breathe the cool mountain air, she would have
recuperated faster. But at that time, the only way to go to the
mountain villages was on horseback. No carriage could get up there—
and there were no cars in those days.

Very few people were left in town. Ramzi's family had also gone to
the mountains. Nouriyeh Hanem was preparing to leave for Antioch.
The heat was really getting unbearable now. Some days, I used to go
to the seashore with my brother or with Nouriyeh Hanem and sit there
until it cooled a little.

I had promised my cousin Marie's husband, Yeghia Effendi, to go
to the mountains with them on Saturday. In the morning he came and
took me there, and I returned with him Monday morning. Up there,
I saw Yeghia Effendi's younger brother, Aram. He was a very serious-
minded and intelligent young man, and it was pleasant to talk to
him.

When I got back, my mother informed me that Nouriyeh Hanem
had been asking for me. The next morning, I went over to Nouriyeh
Hanem's house, and she told me that Farouz Hanem wanted to see me
and that she was on her way.

Farouz Hanem arrived, and after she had kissed me and asked about my mother and my grandmother, she said: "Look, my dear, I came down from the mountains to see you. I want to tell you that I had a frank talk with my son. I thought that keeping your problem a secret from Ramzi would only make things more difficult. I told him quite openly that the problem was that he is Moslem and you are Christian.

"When he heard this, he seemed to change into a statue. He could not say anything; he bent his head and seemed lost in his thoughts. I told him that you would be willing to marry him today but that you did not see how you could set aside your people and convince your family. His eyes filled with tears. I told him not to despair, that nothing was impossible and that he should not lose hope.

"He told me that nothing but death would separate him from you.

"As I explained to my son, I had felt duty bound to discuss these things with my husband first. He has known of your relationship for some time. I told him about meeting you, about our conversation, and why you found it impossible to marry Ramzi. My husband thought you were very wise, and he understood your concerns. We thought of seeking out your mother and brother to talk things over with them and to reveal our son's wish to marry you, but we gave up the idea. Time was very short, and it was not a good time because of your grandmother's illness. I also understand from Nouriyeh Hanem that your poor mother is in the midst of a lot of turmoil because of your brother and that she wants to return to Aintab as soon as possible.

"This did not seem to us like a good time to come with a marriage proposal. We were concerned that if we brought up the prospect of your marriage to our son in the midst of all these difficulties, they would surely turn us down. The problem would then become even more difficult. Ramzi's father asked me to tell both of you to continue your relationship but not to rush things. He promises to do all he can, with the help of God. Through means that are acceptable to your

family, we will see to it that you are united. This is Ramzi's father's message.

"So, my dear, just as I told Ramzi: please wait; place your trust in God and then in us. Just as our son loves you, so do we."

She again kissed and embraced me. I kissed her hand in return and thanked her for being so concerned about me.

Finally, Farouz Hanem said: "Look, my dear. You must have a final meeting with each other. If you both agree that you will wait for each other and remain faithful to each other, you should make a promise before God—and as a sign you should place a ring on each other's finger and leave the future to God. Ramzi is going to travel soon. You, too, will be going away. From here on, your relationship will be by correspondence. My husband has a niece who lives in Aintab. Ramzi can spend at least a month of his summer vacation with her. You can then see each other at her house. God is capable of all things. Remember, as days, months, and years pass, things can change. So I pray for you and wish you success and happiness."

Ramzi's mother then turned to Nouriyeh Hanem and asked her to create another opportunity for Efronia and her son to meet and to become secretly engaged.

14

A Ring for the Road

One day in early August, the doctor came over to examine Trvandah. Although she was still quite weak, he thought she was strong enough to travel and that leaving the unhealthful climate of Iskenderun would be good for her. Not losing one moment, Ovsannah started making her travel arrangements.

Highwaymen and robbers were still a threat to travelers between Iskenderun and Aintab. Ovsannah sent word to old Mule Driver Hagop, who gave in to her pleadings and promised to take them back to Aintab. They set their departure for August 23, 1913.

That wasn't one day too soon for Ovsannah. The whole Iskenderun venture had been a mistake. The climate had exhausted her. Her mother had been seriously ill. Her daughter had been plagued by unsuitable young men. And in spite of their presence, her oldest son had continued his disreputable life. She assumed it would be just a matter of time before he was fired from his job.

There were moments, in the midst of her packing, when she found it a little strange that her daughter Efronia wasn't showing more enthusiasm for returning to Aintab. Could there be some reason for this—something she didn't know about? Ovsannah quickly dismissed the thought. As soon as they got to Aintab, she would contact her cousin's family and have Efronia engaged to the cousin's son. That would be the end of her troubles on that front.

But Efronia had a different idea:

As I already mentioned, I had arrived at my decision the previous night: whatever happened, no matter what difficulties arose, I was going to try to marry Ramzi. And with the help of God, I was going to succeed. I waited for Nouriyeh Hanem to arrange the meeting we had all agreed to.

I did not have to wait long. A few days after my meeting with Farouz Hanem, she sent word that we were to meet at her house. Ramzi was already there when I arrived. He stood up and greeted me. I sensed that he was not quite happy and not in a good mood. He kept looking down. Nouriyeh Hanem sat with us for a while, and then she left us alone.

Ramzi turned to me and knelt down in front of me. He took my hands into his and looked into my eyes. All that he said during that hour, his confessions, his promises—it would take a poet to write down all of the poor boy's expressions of love for me. How can I possibly remember all those words now, when so many years have passed? I cannot.

But I have never forgotten his last words, and I never will. "My beloved and adorable angel," he said. "Only death can separate me from you. Listen to me: I am willing to become a Christian for the sake of your love. I will go to your church, and in front of God and in the presence of your people, I will make my confession and be baptized. I beg you not to refuse me, not to abandon me."

When I saw him in this state, I took him by the hand and made him sit next to me. I looked into his eyes and said: "My darling, I, too, swear to God that only death will separate us; I will not abandon you, and I will not be separated from you. I do not want you to change your religion for my sake or to deny your own faith."

Ramzi joyfully called in Nouriyeh Hanem and told her about the promise we had made to each other. Then all three of us agreed to fulfill his mother's wish by exchanging rings as a sign of our love. We decided to meet four days later at the club.

We parted with happy hearts and with promises to remain faithful to each other, and we left the future to God.

Those four days passed quickly. We went to the club, and in the presence of Ramzi's mother and Nouriyeh Hanem, we placed the rings on each other's fingers. They were lovely rings. The stones were turquoise from Persia and very valuable. Farouz Hanem and Nouriyeh Hanem kissed our cheeks and wished us a happy wedding. We had dinner there, eating and drinking happily. That night, Ramzi and I parted with our hearts full of hope for the future.

Five or six days passed. Most of the people of Iskenderun had already left town. My family made some farewell visits; one of them was to Nouriyeh Hanem. When we arrived, Ramzi was also there. We greeted each other, and my mother asked how his mother was. Then she expressed many thanks to Nouriyeh Hanem for the love and friendship she had shown me.

Later, back at home, I sensed that a suspicion had arisen in my mother's heart on seeing Ramzi there at such an unexpected time. But she said nothing.

In the late afternoon of August 23, two covered wagons arrived in front of our house. Mule Driver Hagop loaded our belongings into one of them and sent it ahead. In the other one he spread some bedding, and my grandmother, my mother, and I climbed in. We took along sufficient food and other belongings for four days.

Saying goodbye to my brother, we started on our way toward Beylan. We planned to spend the night in Beylan because bandits made travel beyond that point dangerous at night. Also, we had some family friends there, and they were expecting us.

We were quite close to Beylan when, all of a sudden, our wagon lurched to one side and stopped. One of the wheels had become caught

95

in a pothole in the road; Mule Driver Hagop could not get it out, no matter how hard he tried. He now regretted that he had sent the other wagon ahead of us. He did not know what to do. He needed to go to Beylan for help—but how could he leave us alone in the middle of nowhere?

Suddenly, in the distance, we heard the galloping of a horse. I immediately knew that it was Ramzi. He got close to us, stopped his horse, and dismounted. It was as if an angel had descended from heaven. He was a sight worth seeing: in his riding clothes, he looked doubly handsome and distinguished.

Ramzi asked Mule Driver Hagop what had happened and if he could be of any help. The man was delighted to see him. "My boy, God Himself must have sent you," he said. "Even though the place the ladies were going to stop for the night is fairly close, the two old ladies cannot walk all the way there; and how can I leave them here alone? I must go to town to bring another wagon for them and get someone who can help me get the wheel out of the hole and fix it."

Ramzi said, "I am going to Kirikhan, but I'm in no hurry. I'll be glad to stay with the ladies until you come back." Hagop was pleased. He mounted one of his horses and headed for town.

Ramzi spoke with my mother in Turkish at some length. Then he and I conversed in English so my mother wouldn't understand. It was unbelievable that Ramzi and I should meet again so soon. We told each other that the hand of Providence must be in this. That renewed our hopes; now we felt certain that God would unite us.

While Ramzi and I walked around and talked, my mother and grandmother spent the time sitting in the stranded wagon. Finally, old Hagop arrived with help, and we proceeded toward Beylan.

When we finally arrived at our relatives' house, they were relieved to see us and welcomed us cordially. Ramzi came in with us. He introduced himself, and my relative, a doctor, recognized his father's name and said, "Give him my regards. Your father is a great man. I have much respect for him." They offered us dinner, but we said we had eaten. We had coffee, and soon after that, Ramzi stood up to leave. As I accompanied him to the door, he told me softly, "Get yourself to the room facing the street so that we can see each other for a few more minutes and talk through the window. I'll be waiting outside."

The doctor and his wife had noticed that we were very tired and showed us to our bedrooms. My mother and grandmother shared one room, and I took the other one. After everyone had said goodnight, I went to the window and opened it. Ramzi came around; he held my hands through the iron grill, and he kissed them. We talked for a while and then said goodbye, but not before he had asked me to write soon. As he rode off, I stood at the window until I could no longer hear the sound of his horse.

We traveled for three more days, spending the nights in the roadside inns, the khans. *Poor Hagop again spent the nights standing guard in front of our door; he hardly got any sleep. On the fourth day we reached the village of Beshgüz, close to Aintab. My brother Yervant, my uncle Hovhannes, and my sister Aroussiak were there to meet us. Happy to be reunited, we embraced each other. When we reached home, there were several other relatives waiting for us, and we all had dinner. I was very happy to see all of them, though I noticed that my brother Yervant had lost a lot of weight. That evening, I was very tired and went straight to bed.*

The following morning when I woke up, I had no idea where I was at first. But then I realized I was back in my old house. I sat in bed for a long time and thought about the eleven months we had spent in Iskenderun, and everything that had happened passed in front of my eyes. I remembered so many things, but it all felt like a dream.

15

Aintab Again

Although Ovsannah felt happy to be free from the miseries of Iskenderun, she soon discovered that Yacoub had been casting a long shadow. Her younger son, Yervant, looked tired and drawn; he had lost a lot of weight. Worse than that, he seemed to have lost all hope for the future. He had worked hard in school and graduated at the top of his class. But the hope that his brother, Yacoub, would help him with the cost of tuition for the Syrian Protestant College in Beirut had come to nothing. He had written Yacoub several times; the letters had gone unanswered. Finally, in a brief letter, his brother had told him bluntly that he could not help him in any way. Yervant then put aside all hopes for a higher education and accepted an offer to teach in a local high school.

By the time Trvandah, Ovsannah, and Efronia got back and were settled, the schools were about to open for the fall term. Efronia wanted to teach, but all the positions were already filled. A few weeks into the term, however, one of the fourth-grade teachers suddenly resigned after receiving an unexpected offer of marriage, and Efronia got the job.

She began work right away. She also joined the Society for the Advancement of Education and the church choir. The combined salaries of Yervant and Efronia were enough to cover the family's expenses, and life for Efronia took on a certain comfortable routine.

But there was one thing to settle. Since her separation from Ramzi, she had written to him several times but not received a single letter in reply. The reason was simple: she did not yet have an address where he could write her and where his letters would safely reach her hands.

She turned to her sister Aroussiak:

My sister Aroussiak and I loved each other dearly. She was liberal-minded, trustworthy, and educated. I thought of meeting with her and revealing all my secrets to her, certain that she would understand my sorrows and that she would help me. Aroussiak, like me, had lived with dreams of marrying a kindred soul, an educated man, someone she could love. But on the contrary, she had been pressured into marrying a rich, stingy, and ignorant man, and she remained unhappy for the rest of her life. So I was certain she would sympathize with my plight and that she would help me.

Taking courage, I opened my heart to her and told her everything: about my falling in love with Ramzi; about our pure and virtuous relationship; about the hardships I had gone through and the difficult situation in which I had placed Ramzi. Finally, through my tears, I confessed our decision to get married when Ramzi finished his education.

Aroussiak listened carefully. When I had finished, she embraced me and told me not to cry. "Sister, do not lose hope," she said. "I will do everything I can for you. Rather than see you unhappily married, I want you to marry someone you love, no matter what his religion."

I immediately sent her address to Ramzi, and his letters began to come. He sometimes answered one of mine with two of his. They were full of joy and hope. And since Ramzi wrote me in English and my sister received many letters from former school friends who wrote to her in English, we felt certain Ramzi's letters would raise no suspicions should Aroussiak's husband see them.

Everything was now in place. The money my brother and I were making sufficed for our needs. My brother was once again hoping to go to Beirut to study, and he was saving some money for that purpose. We felt comfortable and happy. But this did not last long. One never knows what surprises the days will bring.

One day, my mother received a letter from the Katchadourians in Iskenderun. Just seeing the envelope filled her heart with foreboding. The letter read as follows:

Dear Mrs. Ovsannah,

We are writing to tell you that we have been obliged to close down the pharmacy here. We are very sorry to give you this news. There are a few tasks to attend to, after which your son Yacoub will have no further business here and will return to Aintab. Far from helping us make a profit, we are sorry to say he has plunged us into debt.

You must surely have been aware of the kind of life your son was leading during your eleven months here. We waited patiently for two years, partly for your sake and partly to be helpful to him. We feel we have tried, but it has been no use.

The point where we gave up came some time ago. We are sorry to have to tell you this, as we know it will be very painful to you, but a few weeks ago, your son became embroiled in a quarrel at a brothel. He later returned and set fire to the building. The authorities imprisoned him. After much effort and after spreading around a lot of money, we finally got him out of jail.

The letter plunged Osvannah into despair. She had had enough. She said, "I'm going to write to him and ask him not to return to this area. Let him go wherever he wants. Let me not see his face again."

But when Yacoub returned, Ovsannah relented. He was back earlier than expected, looking thin and drawn, ill at ease, and suffering from malaria.

Needless to say, he had no money. But Yervant had a big

heart. Of all the children, he was the one with the most reason to resent his brother. But now, says Efronia, "seeing the condition Yacoub was in, he took pity on him. He had a little drawer where he kept his money. For Yacoub's sake, he would leave it unlocked so that the elder brother could take what he needed without having to ask for it."

There is a saying, writes Efronia, that goes, "His eyes are closed, but his luck is open." And once again, fate seemed to forgive Yacoub. The elderly relative who had paid for Yacoub's education owned several pharmacies in Aintab. One of them was run by a handsome but poor young man who did not have enough money to strike out on his own. One day, an offer arrived for him—with some strings attached: If the young man would consent to marry the oldest daughter of a certain wealthy man, the father of the girl would open a pharmacy for him. The handsome fellow was happy to settle his future in this fashion, and that gave Yacoub a chance to apply for and win his job.

One day in the early spring of 1914, a letter arrived from Ramzi in London. He wrote that his patience was running out; as soon as his school was out for the summer, he was coming straight to Aintab to see Efronia. He wrote:

> My plan was to go to Iskenderun first, and to spend a month with my parents. But I have had to change my mind. Efronia, I have a classmate here who has told me, in all confidence, that a world war is going to break out this summer. It is not clear yet in what month, but it is coming. This friend's father is an army general, and my friend has overheard a conversation that his father had with someone important in his office.
>
> In view of this news, as soon as my school is out—on June 5—I shall immediately get going, God willing. When you were in Iskenderun, my mother mentioned to you that my father has a relative in Aintab whose wife is my cousin. My father has now

written to them and told them I will be spending part of the summer with them. My cousin's name is Münever. I have written to her myself. Her husband's name is Osman Zade Midhad Bey. They are a well-known family. Anyone you ask will be able to point out their house to you. Before I get there, please go and see her. She knows about us.

Efronia immediately ran to her sister. How was she going to find out who these people were?

Aroussiak assured her, "Don't worry, my dear. My brother-in-law is the doctor of all the well-known Moslem families. I can easily find out from him who this family is."

A few days later, in a roundabout way, she asked her brother-in-law about the family.

"I know this family very well," he said. "I'm their family physician. They are rich and well known. They live on Elbehler Street, in a fine, large house. Anyone in the neighborhood can point it out to you."

Aroussiak went and located the house. Not only that; she knocked on the door and asked to see Ramzi's cousin, Münever Hanem. They were very open with each other. The cousin knew everything, and she had heard from Ramzi. As Aroussiak was leaving, Münever Hanem sent her maid along to learn the way to her house, so that she could find it when she came with the news of Ramzi's arrival.

With this, the preparations for Efronia's and Ramzi's reunion were complete. Efronia writes:

Those days passed so slowly. My school was ending in a few days. My eyes were now glued to the road; I was waiting for news. And finally one day, my sister came with word that Ramzi was coming late the following day and that he was expecting us the morning after.

Chapter 15

I cannot describe my happiness. The next morning, I wore a dress that he liked very much and went to fetch my sister, telling my mother that Aroussiak and I would be visiting a friend.

When we entered the large house on Elbehler Street, Ramzi was standing in the spacious living room, looking more handsome than ever.

This was early June 1914. Aintab was at its most beautiful. The first roses of summer were out, and their fragrance mingled with birdsong in the crisp air.

A few weeks later, on June 28, in a town that Efronia had never heard of, a Serbian assassin would raise his gun and kill Archduke Francis Ferdinand of Austria-Hungary. A few weeks after that, declarations of war between countries would follow one another in ever-widening circles, until there was hardly a country or a territory in the world that was not involved in the conflagration.

But on that early June morning Efronia, looking like a bride in her white dress as she walked down Elbehler Street to meet Ramzi, could not have known that time was already running out for the Ottoman Empire and all the Armenians in it.

Ovsannah Finds Out

The house on Elbehler Street was more splendid than anything Efronia had ever seen; in her words, it was "like a palace, the rooms furnished according to the latest mode." A shining samovar, surrounded by many kinds of sweets and cakes, sat on the large table in the living room. Costly Persian rugs covered the floors. At the back of the house was a well-tended garden with fragrant roses and shady trees. Through the half-open French doors came the sounds of a soothing fountain.

As Efronia held Ramzi's hands and looked into his eyes, she felt protected by those beautiful surroundings. What could possibly go wrong now? Ramzi had come. And Aroussiak and Münever Hanem were there, her guardian angels, ready to help her and Ramzi find their future.

For one moment, she forgot her disquietude. She forgot that she had lied and told her mother she was going to visit a friend. For one blissful moment when she was alone with Ramzi in the garden and Ramzi put a gold locket with their pictures around her neck, she felt as if her mother and brothers had seen them and had given them their blessing.

The first few days of Ramzi's visit passed like a dream. Efronia dressed plainly and left her house every morning, giving choir practice as her excuse, but in a bundle under her arm she carried the beautiful dress she was going to change into once she got to her sister's house. There, she changed as quickly as she could and jumped into the carriage that was already waiting to take her to Ramzi.

On the outskirts of the city, Münever Hanem's family had a summer place, a country cottage surrounded by lovely gardens. "It would be superfluous to describe the happy and pleasant times that Ramzi and I spent there," Efronia writes. "We were together almost daily. The summer house was just the sort of place for lovers to be with each other in private. We owed all this to Münever Hanem and to my sister, and we were grateful."

But soon something happened that would break the spell. Efronia continues:

One day, Ramzi and I were sitting in Münever's garden by ourselves. He looked at me in a serious way and said, "Look, my dear. These fifteen days are much too short. I would have liked to spend the whole summer with you. But I am sorry to say I won't be able to stay much longer.

"I received a letter from my father yesterday. He urges me not to delay my return to London much longer and to try to stop and see him and my mother in Iskenderun on my way back. Efronia, the news is bad. My father, who has influential friends, hears things. They say war is going to erupt any day. This is what he writes:"

Ramzi took a letter from his pocket and read:

My dear son—even though we feel happier the longer you stay with your fiancée, we have to face the fact that the Turks are going to enter the war. Quite possibly the roads will be closed, in which case you won't be able to get back to school, and we will be in a state of constant worry. Therefore, your mother and I urge you to meet with your fiancée's family and reveal to them what I am now writing to you in secret about the situation. And, after you have gotten their consent, I urge you to please take her with you to London. My son, this war is going to be very bad for the Armenians. Let her family take pity on that angelic girl, because I fear that many calamities may befall her. Please convey my greetings to them; it makes no sense to keep your relationship a secret from them any longer.

It is not essential even that you get married right away. Tell them you will take her with you as a sister and place her in school in London. Let her continue her education. I will be responsible for all expenses. As I have always told you, we can leave the future to God.

Ramzi folded the letter and told me: "Look my dear, these are my father's wishes. They are also mine. Think hard."

I said, "What can I possibly do? What is there for me to think about? I am ready not only to go to London with you but to the end of the world this very day. If you find it appropriate, let us meet with my sister and see what advice she has to give us."

It was late when I got home. I felt as if I were about to lose my mind. No sleep came across my eyes that night. Everything was easy as far as I was concerned—except how I would tell my family and make them understand.

The next morning, I went to my sister and told her what Ramzi's father had suggested. My sister looked at me. She was startled. What could she say?

She was quiet for a moment. "Look, dear sister," she said at last. "I don't think it is right to keep this problem a secret from our mother any longer. I now feel obliged to let her know everything. Let's send the maid for her right away and hear what she will say. It's no use for me to talk to Ramzi before we have met with Mother."

I agreed with her. We sent the maid over to fetch my mother.

She came right away, looking alarmed and wondering why we had sent for her so suddenly. Aroussiak took a deep breath and said:

"I have no good news, Mother. We asked you to come here so that we could tell you about the difficulties and the sufferings, the secrets *and the anguish that your daughter has been going through for months. We hope that, as her mother, you can alleviate the sufferings and the wounds of her heart.*

"Look, dear Mother. My sister, your daughter, fell in love with a young man in Iskenderun and has been carrying on a relationship with him for some time now. They are very much in love. She has sworn not to marry anyone but this young man. They both claim that only death will separate them.

"The young man is now here in Aintab. After studying in London this past year, he has come all the way here to see her. I went with her to see him. Mother, what a young man! His conversation is so pleasant! In all my life I have never seen such a handsome and gracious person. It is obvious that he is a highly decent young man."

My mother cut her short: "So tell me who this young man is."

I had kept quiet until then. But now I said, "You know him very well, Mother. He is the son of Nouriyeh Hanem's relatives. You saw him at her house, as well as on the day of his graduation."

She stopped and thought. Then she remembered and said, "So far as I recall, the boy is a Persian Moslem." She then turned to me and said, "My suspicions have proved correct. My daughter, you are an Armenian. How could you fall in love with a Moslem and wish to marry him? You kept going to Nouriyeh Hanem's house day and night and accompanied her to the club. So this is what was behind it all!"

I interrupted her and said: "Mother, please do not get angry or blame me for this matter. I do not have the heart to bear it. Yes, I love him. We fell in love, and I want to marry him. He is such a decent and saintly boy that there is not one like him among all your Protestants. I have known him for many months. Not once has an immoral word come out of his mouth nor has he ever held my hand with a bad intention. He has dealt with me as he would with his sister. He is an angel. Let me make it short: I swear before God and before both of you that only death will separate us from each other.

Either I will marry this young man, or I will not marry at all. I will become a Catholic nun."

I began to cry. "Don't say anything more," I continued, "and don't ask any further questions. Think about it. Hasn't my sister already told you about his father's letter? I fear things will happen that you will come to regret. But by then it would be of no avail. Mother, I beg you to send me with him to London. Who, I ask you, is going to find out that I have gone there with him? To those who ask, simply say you have sent me there to study. And it wouldn't be a lie, since his father is more than happy to let me study in London. He promises to take care of all my expenses.

"Mother, you can be certain that he will take better care of me than my own brothers. We will each pursue our education for a few years, and then we shall see what God will ordain. I shall not say another word. You should only know that if you do not give your consent, I will be unhappy for the rest of my life, and your conscience will torment you."

Throughout this outburst, my mother had remained quiet. I sobbed: "Mother, do you really think I would marry your cousin's son? What right did you have to promise me to his mother on her deathbed, when I was still young, without my consent? I heard he has returned from Beirut with his diploma. It will not be long before they come with their proposal; I am sure of that. Let me tell you right now that I will never marry him, even if God takes my soul away."

I cried so hard then that my sister felt sorry for me, as well as for my mother. She said, "This is enough for today. Give Mother a chance to think about it, and we shall meet again."

I had promised to see Ramzi the next day, and there was no longer any need to keep my visits a secret from my mother. I did not go home that night, but stayed at my sister's house.

When Aroussiak and I arrived at Münever Hanem's house the next day, Ramzi was already there, waiting for us. My sister told *him about our meeting with our mother, what Mother had said, and how I answered her. Then she said, "I am sorry I could not be more helpful to you. I trust that God will grant your wish and join you and my sister. I agree with your and your father's wishes, and I can assure you I will do everything I can to send my sister to study with you. By the time both of you complete your studies, who knows what surprises may have occurred and what changes may have taken place. God is great."*

Ramzi was very sad, and very moved. That evening, he accompanied us in his carriage to my sister's house and then went back to Münever Hanem's. My sister took me home since I was still very angry with my mother and would not speak to her. Aroussiak told her about our visit with Ramzi. She brought up the issue of my going to London with Ramzi again but still found it impossible to convince my mother. Finally, my mother said, "If you wish, and if you both find it suitable, let me discuss this with my sons. Whatever happens, one day they may hear about it, and then they will be upset with me that I did not discuss the matter with them."

I did not want her to do this. "Ramzi asked to speak to you and to my brothers, but I would not let him," I said. "I know very well how unreasonable they are, especially Yacoub. I was afraid they would say all sorts of foolish things and throw in his face the fact that he is a Moslem. I don't want him to be hurt or upset. I will leave it to God to ordain the best."

Our fifteen days went by very fast. Ramzi was going to start his journey one morning at eight o'clock. We spent the day before his departure together. Although we were both trying to be happy, it was impossible. The pain of separation was in our hearts. That day, Münever Hanem's husband came to lunch, and we ate together. Later, Ramzi took me to his room, where he had packed everything for his departure. He again brought up my mother's refusal to let me go to London.

"My love," he said. "My mind is not at ease as I leave you. I'm

going to worry about you day and night. Your mother is taking the wrong step. When war breaks out, who is going to keep you safe here? Who knows what calamities the Turks are going to bring down on the heads of the Armenians? I pray to God that He will keep you from danger."

Early the next morning, Ramzi came and picked me up from my sister's house. The carriages were ready. We were going to accompany him to a village just outside of town, Beshgüz—the same village where my sister had met me when we arrived from Iskenderun. Münever Hanem and her children got into their carriage, and Ramzi and I got into the carriage in which he was going to travel.

When we got to Beshgüz, we sat in a café and had a cup of coffee. Later, as Ramzi got back into his carriage, he looked into my eyes. His last words to me were in English. Embracing me, he said: "My angel, will I ever be able to find you again?"

He took out his handkerchief and dried my tears. Then he got into the wagon, and it took off. He waved his handkerchief at us until he no longer could be seen. As I stood there, at that moment, I had a presentiment that this was to be our last meeting.

Efronia's family before she was born, Aintab, 1892. Left to right, in the back, Ovsannah, Aroussiak, Yacoub, and Kevork. Center, Azniv. On Kevork's lap, Yervant.

Efronia with some of her kindergarten classmates. She is in the top
row against the door, with her hand to her cheek. The girl on the
left of her (that is, to her right), is Yester, her future sister-in-law
who would marry Yacoub.

The church choir, Aintab, ca. 1911. Efronia is in the front row at the far left. Next to her is her brother Yervant.

The Sunday school teachers, Aintab, 1912. Efronia is in the rear center.

Efronia's family, 1914. Left to right, Yervant, Azniv, Efronia, Ovsannah, Aroussiak, Yacoub.

Efronia and Aram in Beirut, 1923.

Efronia holding Herant in his baptismal dress, Iskenderun, 1933.

Efronia in California, spring 1986. She died on December 30 of that year.

A page from Efronia's manuscript.

Efronia's family tree.

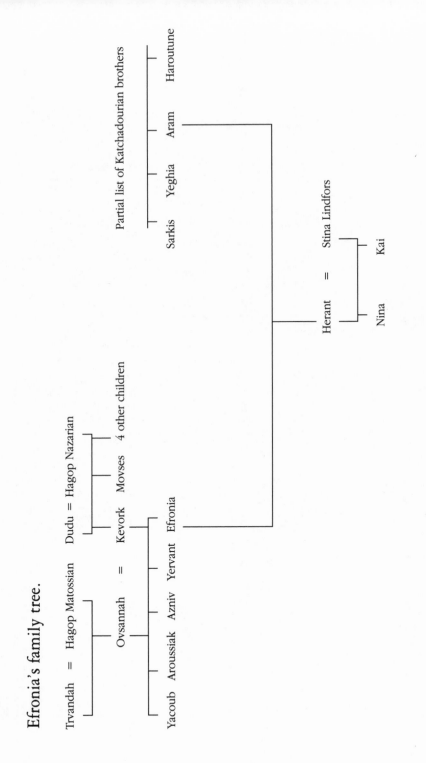

Partial list of Katchadourian brothers

Sarkis   Yeghia   Aram   Haroutune

Trvandah = Hagop Matossian   Dudu = Hagop Nazarian

Ovsannah =   Kevork   Movses   4 other children

Yacoub   Aroussiak   Azniv   Yervant   Efronia

Herant = Stina Lindfors

Nina   Kai

Part III

DARKNESS
IN ANATOLIA

Darkness Descends

Ramzi's father was right: there was a war on the horizon. In Europe a delicate balance of power was being threatened. France's defeat in the Franco-Prussian War of 1870 had left her thirsting for revenge. The Triple Entente, formed in 1907 by England, France, and Russia, appeared to be an open threat to the German Kaiser. He, in turn, made matters worse by pushing his railroad project in Asiatic Turkey, which was going to connect Berlin to Baghdad in a grand, Eastern power grab. For this, he cultivated and won Turkey's friendship. And that meant that the Armenian population of the Caucasus found itself on both sides of the great power divide: some of them on the Turkish side, others on the Russian.

That was not a good position to be in for a minority in a decaying empire where a new national consciousness was also emerging: a "Pan-Turkism" that was proclaiming the union of all Turkish-speaking peoples and a Greater Turkey for the Turks. By implication, this meant hostility toward non-Turkish minorities. Over the years, the character of Ottoman Turkey had been changing, as more and more pieces of it fell away in the Balkans, North Africa, and the Caucasus. Finally, only one sizable minority remained within its borders—from the Ottoman perspective, the most troublesome of them all: the Armenians.

For more than twenty-five hundred years, the Armenians

had lived on the high plateau between the Black Sea and the Caspian Sea, in an area on both sides of the present Armenian-Turkish border. Down through the centuries, they were forced to defend their land against invaders from all directions, while managing to retain their own distinct culture. For a brief time, during the reign of Tigranes the Great in the first century B.C., they were a major power in the area. By the fourth century, the Armenians had adopted Christianity as a state religion. But by the time they came under the Ottoman Empire in the sixteenth century, their political importance had declined, and they had a long experience of persecution as a religious minority.

But their second-class citizenship and their heavy taxes under the Ottoman sultans did not prevent them, as Efronia's story shows us, from retaining strong community ties. The Armenians in Turkey were competent and hard-working; they were often prosperous artists, merchants, and traders, who were open to contacts with the Western world. In Constantinople, Armenians had both wealth and influence in government and civil service, and many were eminent in the city's cultural life. But most of the Ottoman Armenians were peasants toiling in hundreds of villages spread over the high Anatolian plateau, concerned with little else than how to put bread on the table.

It was into this world that the Protestant missionaries arrived.

By the Ottoman Empire's final days, British, German, and American missionaries had been working there for a century. They eventually established several hundred mission stations all over the empire. They founded schools, hospitals, and colleges. In the Armenians, who by most accounts numbered around 2.5 million before the First World War, they found a people who were very receptive both to their religious teachings and to their progressive Western ideas in general—a fact that made the Turks even more nervous about having Armenians within their borders. And when the war came, these missionaries out in the field became witnesses, not to the glory of God, as they had hoped, but to what seemed to many of them as His fury—brought down, for unfathomable reasons, upon the very people they had hoped to save. What these missionaries saw and what they lived through, they passed on: in letters to their families, in reports to their headquarters, in personal accounts to their ambassadors and other foreign office personnel, in talks with reporters, in their memoirs.

After Ramzi left Aintab, Efronia fell into despair. No matter how she looked at it, the obstacles in the way of her happiness with Ramzi seemed insurmountable. She felt certain that her family, and especially her mother, would remain dead set against her marrying Ramzi. She felt she had only one alternative: to go ahead without their blessing.

While Ramzi was making his way back to London, writing faithfully to Efronia from everywhere he stopped, the old familiar problem of suitors resurfaced.

Efronia had no trouble turning most of them down. But then there was Garabed, the son of Ovsannah's cousin, and Ovsannah's promise to his mother to marry Efronia to him once he had finished his education. Having returned from the Syrian Protestant College in Beirut, he was working as a surgeon at the American hospital in Aintab.

Garabed was ready to get married.

The story of Garabed followed the usual pattern: visits by the relatives, increasingly frequent visits by the young man himself. Ovsannah even consented to visit the family with her daughter. It was all Efronia could do not to show that she was being dragged there against her will. The family began to grow impatient for an answer.

"Look, my daughter," Ovsannah implored. "You saw with your own eyes what a fine family they are. He is a good man. These days, a doctor could ask for the hand of anyone, and her family would immediately give her to him. What do you think?"

Efronia looked away and did not answer.

That same day, the women in the church choir were going for a picnic in a local park. As Efronia was leaving the house, Ovsannah reminded her not to be home late; Garabed's family was coming for a visit that evening. Since they lived on the same street, she had to pass their house on her way to the park. Garabed's older brother, Hagop, was standing outside their house when she passed. He asked Efronia where she was going so early in the morning.

"The church choir is going for a picnic," she answered.

"The white shawl you're wearing isn't appropriate for that. I urge you to go home right away and exchange it for a black one."

She stomped home, changed her shawl, and angrily told her mother, "You insist that I marry their son, and his brother is already ordering me around."

One did not do that lightly with Efronia.

The picnic was wonderful: the women in the church choir spent a delightful afternoon beside a stream in the shady park, enjoying the food and drink and each other's company. But when they returned to town, there was commotion everywhere. People were milling about in the streets, talking agitatedly to each other. Chants of "Allah-u akbar!"—God is great—echoed from minaret to minaret. The town criers were running around shouting, "Compatriots, long life to all Turks; let's march against the enemy."

Efronia's heart sank. Was this the war Ramzi had been talking about? What would happen to them all now? To the Armenians, to her and Ramzi?

She pushed through the crowds and rushed home as fast as she could. When she got there, she found her brothers very agitated; they explained that war had broken out in Europe and that Turkey was mobilizing. The Turkish authorities were not yet recruiting Armenians as soldiers, but all Armenian physicians were being called up and ordered to report for duty in three to four days, along with the Turkish recruits.

Efronia writes about the months that followed:

After the soldiers left, near the end of August, the city gradually calmed down and life went on. The schools opened in September. My brother Yervant and I began teaching at our respective schools, as before. During September, Ramzi's letters began to arrive from London. He was successful in school, but he constantly worried about me. The war was upon us: what would happen to the Armenians: What would happen to me?

We sensed that the Turks were not well disposed toward us. We started hearing rumors about terrible things happening to Armenians elsewhere, about deportations and massacres of the rural population. It was hard to know what to believe. In Aintab things went on as always; people went about their business. But it was not long before everything changed.

Young Armenian men began to be called up for military service. Those who had the means saved their sons by paying an exemption fee. Those who could not pay had to turn themselves in. The Armenians fell to grief and mourning. The schools closed down. Armenians were forbidden to leave the city. All communications with the outside were prohibited also—even the writing and receiving of letters.

Thus a curtain came down between Efronia, in Anatolian Turkey, and Ramzi, thousands of miles away in London, which was now the capital of an enemy power.

It is easy to imagine the effect that news reports from Turkey were having on him. Turkey had entered the war in November. During those first few months an estimated 250,000 young Armenian men were recruited into the Turkish army as regular soldiers to serve alongside the Turks. But soon the Armenians were disarmed and formed into special "work battalions," where they were maltreated and eventually liquidated.

Ominous reports were beginning to trickle into the European and American press. As early as December 5, 1914, the *New York Times* reported on the terrible conditions in the Ottoman Empire:

> Everything is in confusion, trade is utterly paralyzed, travel is impossible, transportation is stopped, schools are stripped of their teachers, money has ceased to circulate, drafts cannot be cashed, grain remains unthreshed and unwinnowed for lack of men and animals to do the work; the labor market is closed. . . .

A few weeks later, on January 12, the London *Morning Post* ran a story with the headline "Christians in Great Peril," quoting Talaat Bey, the Turkish minister of the interior, as saying that "in Turkey henceforth there will be room only for Turks."

At about the time of that article, Efronia's letters to Ramzi stopped. She had had no way of alerting him that communication from the interior of Anatolia had been cut off. Ramzi was now forced to follow the unfolding of his most dreaded nightmare in the London papers.

There had been a real change of heart in the leadership of the Young Turks, who in 1909 had deposed Sultan Abdul Hamid. Initially, Enver, Talaat, and Djemal Pasha, the leaders of this new Ottoman government, espoused liberal, egalitarian ideas, but now they were sounding increasingly intolerant of minorities within the boundaries of the Ottoman Empire. It was no longer a question of limited harassment and small-scale massacres in order to teach the minorities a lesson, as had been the case under Sultan Abdul Hamid II. Their aim was far more sinister: to put an end to the bothersome Armenian problem once and for all by annihilating the Armenians.

If there had been any doubts about the way things were going for the Armenians, they were laid to rest on April 24, 1915. On that day, in Constantinople, the Ottoman Turkish authorities rounded up more than 250 Armenian luminaries— most of the leading writers, politicians, educators, and religious leaders—and sent them to the interior of Turkey, where all of them were put to death. In addition, thousands of Armenians in Constantinople were thrown in jail. The Armenian people now had to face the leadership of the Sublime Porte, as the Ottoman government was called, with the leaders of their community gone and with their young men of fighting age rapidly being killed off in the special labor battalions.

The deportations now began in earnest. Between May and October 1915, in carefully timed stages, most of the Armenian population of Ottoman Turkey was put on the road and forced to march in convoys toward the Syrian desert. Not many made it to their destination, and most of those who did died of starvation, disease, or outright murder on the banks of the Euphrates River at Deir Zor.

There was a general pattern to these mass deportations, as documented in numerous personal accounts and formal reports. Typically, a segment of the Armenian population of a town or that of a whole village would be given notice to move as a convoy "to safer areas until the end of the war." The time allowed to prepare for this march would vary from several days to a few hours. Sometimes people were taken away from their homes and places of work with barely enough time to change clothes for the journey.

The convoys usually consisted of women, children, and old men. Moving toward Deir Zor through the countryside under the blistering sun, they traveled roads lined with Armenian corpses.

What Ramzi was able to gather from the London papers told the story of a government that had unleashed all its fury on a defenseless part of its own population. "Whole Plain Strewn by Armenian Bodies," said one headline. "Armenian Horrors Grow," said another. "Armenians Sent to Perish in Desert" and "Turks Depopulate Towns of Armenia," said two others.

Over and over again, the accounts echo this *New York Times* story of September 15, 1915:

> The deliberate murder of a nation is taking place in this twentieth century. Turkey is now in the act of murdering Armenia, and she has almost completed her work. There are no able-bodied male Armenians left anywhere in Turkey. They have either been brought to an end in the ranks of the Turkish Army, into which they are dragged, or have perished in prisons or at the gallows—the best of them in the latter manner. The remainder of the Armenian nation, composed of women, children, and old men, have been driven out of their homes; towns and cities have been completely depopulated of their Armenian inhabitants, in most instances amounting to thousands in number. They are driven out on a two months' journey on foot, with

no more definite destination than Arabia. Two-thirds of them perish on the way, either from exposure or at the hands of raping and plundering Mohammedans. These reports are from missionaries, Consuls, and Red Cross nurses of other nations.

This state of affairs is the natural course of the Turkish Government's openly expressed policy. What is to be done? Is humanity so situated as to see deliberate murder committed? And on such a scale?

Ambassador Morgenthau is reported to have done his utmost to stave off such happenings, but without avail.

Marooned in London, Ramzi read the papers with mounting despair.

He was reading how they took the pretty girls first, those gendarmes and local rabble and criminals who had been let out of prisons for this very purpose. They sorted out the pretty Armenian girls from the convoys. At night, after they had been marching for hours under the scorching sun with no food and nothing to drink and sometimes naked, they took them out and raped them and then killed them. Some of the women threw themselves into the rivers from bridges, the papers reported, or threw their babies into the rivers to end their suffering. Ramzi read about women who smeared their faces with mud and ashes to look old and ugly; about women who went mad, women who were taken to local harems or sold to villagers for a pittance, and women who ended up along the banks of the Euphrates near Deir Zor, in the Arabian desert, emaciated ghosts left there to die next to the river, which at times was so full of floating bodies that the water hardly moved.

Ramzi read all this, and Efronia's angelic face with the large hazel eyes kept haunting him, day and night.

18

God Doesn't Understand Armenian

One evening in California when Efronia's grandson Kai, then seven, was sleeping over at *Medzmama's* house, he could hear her mumbling in the dark of the bedroom.

He was puzzled: *"Medzmama,* who are you talking to?"

"I'm talking to God, my dear. I'm praying."

"But you speak Armenian. This is America, *Medzmama.* God doesn't understand Armenian."

When the deportations from Aintab began, Efronia may well have wondered whether God did understand Armenian. She never forgot that winter:

In the dead of winter refugees began to arrive in Aintab from Zeitoun, Marash, and their neighboring Armenian villages. These Armenians had left almost everything behind and were carrying only immediate necessities on their backs. They had no idea where they were headed next. Tents were set up in an open field on the outskirts of the city, and there they spent a few days.

We went there to see them. They had left their homes only a few days before, but they were already in so pitiful a state that it is impossible to describe. Children and adults, the old and the sick— how were they all going to be able to continue? They all cried to God to come to their aid. With no idea of what was in store for them, childless people from Aintab took young children to adopt them; those who had no servants took in young women as maids. Mothers were pleading with people to take their children so that at least the children would be saved from this torment. The refugee convoys kept coming for several weeks. And then the deportation of the Armenians of Aintab itself began. The first to go were the families of the Apostolic church, particularly the wealthier, better educated people. Word was sent to a number of families to be ready to leave in a few days. Terror set in. The Armenians brought down into the streets any items they could sell at very cheap prices. But who would want to buy them? The Turks knew well that sooner or later all that belonged to the Armenians would be theirs. The two town criers called out: "People, don't be afraid. Close your doors, put your money in the banks or entrust it to your Turkish friends. It will not be long before you come back. The government assures you."

But who could believe them? Yet there was nothing anyone could do. Convoy after convoy began to leave, led by a few gendarmes. A rumor circulated, claiming that the Protestants were not going to be deported. But soon they, too, had to leave.

I will never forget the fear and trembling during the Sunday church service on the last day before the first Protestant convoy was to leave. The choir sang a few songs. Everyone was crying. Following the worship, those who would be leaving the next day embraced the others tearfully and bade them farewell.

I used to keep a diary at that time, and I took it with me to California. As I look at the pages, I can see tear stains on the paper. Here is some of what I wrote:

> *July 21: The sad news of what is happening now is so painful. May God save us from these dangers. I always want to believe in Him, and I do believe He will rescue us. O my God, have pity on us, we have no other master. Pity us, deliver us, send your angels to guard us . . .*

> *July 22: Jeremiah 31:3, 49:11. Today is one of my very sad days. My face is long, and my heart is in turmoil. Many sorrows and thoughts torment my heart. My tears are close to my eyelashes. The*

rumors about deportations upset me very much. I am so frightened. I
always think about it. I have a headache because of all these worries.
To get away for a while, I am going to church . . .

   August 7: Today is Sunday. I went to Bible study. O my Lord,
what a scene. The whole church is in mourning. Every eye is full of
tears . . . We rehearsed three hymns. We are going to separate tomorrow
from our choir director, who has been working with us for so long.
   After Bible study I went to my sister's house. There were a lot of
people. They are making preparations. Oh, we did not stop crying . . .
There was a lot to do, but I went to church. This would be the last
service. Communion service was in progress when I arrived. I have never
seen so much crying. We sang the hymns. The last hymn was "God Be
with You Until We Meet Again." I could only sing the first two verses.
I could not sing the rest. Tears were running down my face. I covered
my face with my shawl and stood there. Then I sat down. The whole
choir began to sob. How could we help it . . . ?

Efronia herself, although very much part of the Protestant
community, was exceptionally lucky. Thanks to her cousin,
Dr. Hovsep, who was the personal physician of the military
governor, she and her immediate family were exempted from
deportation. Some other family members had also managed to
escape the deportation orders: Efronia's brother Yacoub, on
the basis of his job as the municipal pharmacist, was allowed
to stay in Aintab. So was her sister Aroussiak, whose brother-
in-law had been sent to the front as a physician, which meant
that Aroussiak's husband was assigned to look after the physician's family, as well as his own. Yervant, Efronia's younger
brother, deserted from the army and went into hiding at
Ovsannah's house. It was an extremely risky thing to do. Had
he been discovered, it would have spelled certain exile and
probably death for Efronia and her mother.
   But Efronia's sister Azniv and her family had no way of

protecting themselves from the dreaded order. She was told to prepare for the road:

My sister Azniv and her family were to leave the morning after the church service, so after the service we went directly to her house and spent the night there.

That day's convoy was one of the largest, with some two thousand people in it. The confusion was impossible to imagine. Fortunately, this convoy was sent toward Arab towns and villages like Hama, Homs, and Damascus where the Arabs took good care of the Armenian refugees towns. My sister and her family lived in Damascus until the end of the war. This convoy turned out to be the luckiest group. Following them, all the other convoys that left Aintab were headed to the desert near Deir Zor, and virtually all of them were massacred amid unimaginable tortures.

The evacuation of the Aintab Armenians took several months. We lived confined to our houses. Armenian women veiled themselves like Turks. My brother Yervant was like a prisoner at home.

In spite of all this, Efronia and her family felt extremely fortunate. All they needed to do now, they reasoned, was to sit tight and wait for the war to end. And then, Efronia tried to tell herself, everything would be well. Ramzi would be waiting for her. They would get married. Life would begin.

But once again, Yacoub took a disastrous step. This time, it left Efronia looking straight into the abyss.

19

Yacoub Invites Disaster

By the time the Armenians were being deported from Aintab, Yacoub seemed to have lost his penchant for getting into trouble. Even Ovsannah dared to hope that her elder son had finally calmed down.

Maybe, Ovsannah told herself, she could now count on him to behave in a way befitting his position as the head of the family: as the one ultimately responsible for the welfare of all its members, the one who would maintain order in the family and be the family's spokesman. Yacoub remained self-centered, rarely asking whether his family needed anything, but at least, Ovsannah told herself, he was staying out of trouble. His work as a municipal pharmacist was going smoothly. He cultivated many friends among high-ranking Turkish government officials, especially military officers, and he often brought them home for dinner. On those occasions, Yervant took refuge in his hiding place in the attic, and Efronia stayed out of sight. She writes:

We got used to this life. We thought things would go on in this fashion until the war ended. No matter what difficulties we encountered, we did not mind them, in view of what we heard was happening elsewhere.

It is usually wrong to ascribe the misfortunes in life to fate alone. More often, a man brightens or darkens his fate himself. My foolish brother, for instance, blackened his fate with his own hands; but God helped and saved us. My brother took such a foolish step that only God could save us—with the help of my cousin, Dr. Hovsep. Otherwise, we would have drawn our last breath in Deir Zor.

While we were in Iskenderun, my brother had become engaged to a girl by the name of Yester. Both my mother and I were unhappy with the engagement. My mother did not find the family suitable; I did not like the girl, who had been my classmate all through school. However, we said nothing to Yacoub about all this, and my mother only advised him to think carefully before he married her. Eventually, he changed his mind and broke off the engagement, and my mother and I were very happy.

Yester had three brothers. All of them were experts in the making of a cotton fabric called alajah; *they were famous for their work. All the Armenian artisans who had been doing this work in Urfa had been deported, which meant there was no one left in that town who could produce this material. To correct this, the government ordered Yester's brothers to move to Urfa and to continue their trade there.*

This they were glad to do. They could continue their business, and they would be working under the protection of the government. But they had an unmarried sister, and they were afraid she would be taken from them. They called my brother Yacoub and offered him 150 gold sovereigns if he would reconsider and marry Yester. And my brother agreed, without thinking of the consequences.

When my brother told my mother about his decision, she was shocked. She sent him to talk it over with Dr. Hovsep, who strongly advised him against the marriage. The girl was not a suitable match for Yacoub, he maintained, and in addition, the fact that she was the daughter of a family about to be relocated could cause trouble. But my brother would listen neither to my mother nor to Dr. Hovsep. He thought only about the money. He decided to marry Yester in a big public ceremony.

When we learned of this, it was as if lightning had struck our heads. Was this a time to get married? And could he not at least get married quietly? After his wedding ceremony, Yacoub arranged a feast in our courtyard. He had music blasting out of a gramophone and he carried on as if these were ordinary times.

A few days later, on a Sunday, a few of our friends and relatives who were left in town came to our house to congratulate him. Suddenly, there were knocks on the door, and some thirty armed Turkish soldiers entered. My brother Yervant immediately ran to his hiding place, and I ran to the attic to hide myself, as well. A few of the soldiers came into the house from the courtyard. They searched the men, and then they tied Yacoub's hands and took him away to jail.

It is impossible to imagine that scene. My mother and my grandmother were crying. The new bride was tearing at her hair. Dr. Hovsep came over and saw our condition. He was quite angry with my brother, but it was no use—what was done, was done.

Two days later, the dreadful news came. We received orders that our entire family was to be deported to Deir Zor, the men and the women separately. We cried day and night. We knew for certain that we were going to our deaths.

Following the evacuation of the Armenians, the governor—the Vali—had been replaced. The new governor was a harsh man who spread terror all around. There were some Armenians left in town who had managed not to get deported by bribing government officials. They were hiding in their homes. This new governor had their houses searched, ferreted them all out, and deported them. He was an army officer who had fought in the war and been shot in the kidney. An able man, he had been discharged from the military and appointed governor of Aintab. Although he had already had his surgery before he came, his wounds still needed dressing and care. Having heard there was a famous doctor in the American Hospital, he had sought this doctor's services. The physician in question was my cousin, Dr. Hovsep, who treated him from then on.

The governor was very pleased with Dr. Hovsep and had grown very fond of him. After this calamity burst over our heads, Dr. Hovsep had once again gone to dress the governor's wounds. When he was done, he addressed the governor in a very sweet voice:

"My Bey, I have a favor to ask of you."

"Doctor," interrupted the governor, "you had better ask me something that I can or would want to do for you."

"I am sure you recall," said my uncle, "how angry and upset you were—and rightly so—when a few days ago an Armenian man was making a public spectacle of his wedding. You had the young man arrested, and you ordered his family to be deported. My Bey, they are my uncle's family. Their son has taken a very bad step, and you are entitled to punish him. But I beg you, my Bey, for the love of God, to take back the order to deport them."

The governor was silent for a long time. Then he said: "It is hard for me to rescind my order. But as a favor to you I will do what I can to save the family from deportation. However, as soon as the young man gets out of jail, he will have to be sent away."

The governor ordered my brother to be sent to the nearby region of Roumeliye, only a few hours away from Aintab. We decided my grandmother should go along to look after him, so the poor old woman got herself ready to go. As soon as my brother got out of jail, the mules were brought over, and they left immediately. As if all the troubles he had caused earlier were not enough—this added salt and pepper to our wounds. And apart from our own sorrows, we now had to listen to the crying and wailing of his bride all day long.

Barely fifteen days passed after Yacoub's departure when in the middle of the night we heard a knock on the door. My mother opened it, and there was my brother. We all ran downstairs. Yacoub had left our grandmother behind and had made it back, intending to stay for a few days.

Word of his absence from Roumeliye had already been reported to the authorities. Dr. Hovsep also heard about it and came running to our house. He scolded my brother severely. A while later, my brother began to vomit. It turned out that when he heard that word of his escape had reached the government, he had become so frightened that he had gone to his room and taken poison.

The poor doctor stayed with him until morning and treated him in various ways. He made him vomit, fed him yogurt, and after this and all sorts of other treatments, my brother felt a bit better. Early in the morning, before sunrise, he was put on his horse and sent away.

In the morning, the police came to arrest him, but they could not find him anywhere. We told them they must have gotten the wrong information. "He never came here," we said.

Some four or five months later, the governor was replaced again. Our cousin Hagop Effendi appealed to several government officials for my brother's return, saying they needed him in the municipal pharmacy. Eventually, my brother was pardoned. He returned home and went back to work.

The calamities and fears because of Yacoub affected us profoundly. At the same time, life at home became more and more difficult. My brother Yervant was still confined to the house. The four of us were now dependent on my brother Yacoub and his wife, Yester. We began to realize that Yester did not look upon us kindly.

We had often heard that Yester's mother made life difficult for her daughters-in-law; now Yester was treating us the same way. There was a vast difference between our family and hers. The members of our immediate family—and even our entire lineage—dealt with each other with civility, love, and respect. In Yester's family, there was constant fighting and commotion, as if they were each other's enemies. The wives of Yester's three brothers never had a day of peace. I regret very much that my sister-in-law continued to lead that same kind of life. She showed respect for neither young nor old. When it was time for my brother to come home from work, she would get all dressed up and make herself look pretty. With such empty means, she would try to win my brother's love. When my brother was drinking, she would try to turn him against us by complaining about us. With false words and to no good purpose, she would try to create misunderstandings.

But no matter what she said or did, we would respond with only silence and patience. We did not want discord in our house. However, silence and patience were of little use. As they say in Turkish, "She turned the food we ate into poison."

My poor brother Yervant would see all this and get very perturbed. Sometimes we considered living separately from my brother and his wife, so that even if we had to live on dry bread, we would at least have peace. But we were not certain we could manage. Life had become very expensive.

Finally, Yervant became so exasperated with the situation at home that he turned himself in to the authorities. He was sent to Aleppo. We were very saddened by the separation. Yet at the same time we were glad he would no longer have to witness the plight of his family, who in the past, even in the midst of poverty and helplessness, had always managed to live happily. As he was about to leave, he turned to us with tears in his eyes and said, "I will worry about you. I know that life is a torment for you. But don't be sad. I hope to return safe and sound, and to support you comfortably."

Life at home now became intolerable. We lost all our freedom. From morning till night we were busy with housework. We were constantly under my sister-in-law's command. And even though my brother supported us, we still had many unmet needs. Yacoub and Yester never thought about these needs, so my mother, who knew how to spin cotton and had a spinning wheel, began to buy cotton, spin it, and sell her work at the marketplace to peasants who used it to weave a special cloth called bez, from which they made their underwear. In this way, my mother was able to make some money as well as distract herself a little.

I decided that, since the schools were closed, I would gather the children of the nearby families who were still in town and teach them. So I sent word to our neighbors and got together twelve boys and girls around the age of ten. I held my classes in the mornings. I got some satisfaction out of this, although I had little enthusiasm for it. But at least my pupils allowed me to forget myself for a while.

Little did I know that my little private school would also allow me to get in touch with my beloved Ramzi again.

News from Ramzi

All through the summer and into the fall of 1915, the deportations and massacres continued. In carefully timed stages, moving from one region to another, the Armenian population was put on the road. Of the larger cities, only Constantinople, Smyrna, and Aleppo were spared wholesale eviction. The German pastor Johannes Lepsius's book from 1919, *Le Rapport Secret*, contains a long list of dates and localities from which the convoys started. The Armenians of Erzerum were deported on June 15; Harput and Trebizond followed on June 26. On July 28, with Efronia as an eyewitness, the first convoys left Aintab. On August 16, it was the turn of Marash and Konya. On August 19, deportation orders were issued in Urfa, and then Izmit, Bursa, Barzidag, Adazapari, and the surrounding regions, during the week starting on August 10. And so it went, until there were hardly any towns or villages left that had not been touched by the orders issuing from the office of the minister of interior, Talaat Pasha, and from the War Ministry under Enver Pasha.

By early summer, any efforts on the part of the Ottoman government to keep its Armenian policy secret from the world had proven to be in vain. Britain, France, and Russia claimed knowledge of the widespread massacres of Armenians as early as May 1915 and threatened to hold the Ottoman government responsible. This had no effect: in the provinces, the convoys kept marching to their deaths. In Constantinople, U.S. Ambassador Henry Morgenthau tried every conceivable way he could think of to stop the carnage. In his book, *Ambassador Morgenthau's Story*, he provides a chilling insight into the minds of the Young Turk triumvirate.

"Why are you so interested in the Armenians anyway?" Talaat Pasha asked Morgenthau one day, according to the book. "You are a Jew; these people are Christians. The Mohammedans and the Jews always get on harmoniously. . . . Why can't you let us do with these Christians as we please?"

At one point during an audience with Enver Pasha, Morgenthau suggested that the reports of massacres surely were exaggerated and that they must be the work of local people. Not so, replied Enver, refusing to grab this chance to exonerate himself.

"You are greatly mistaken," said Enver. "We have this country absolutely under our control. I have no desire to shift the blame on to our underlings and I myself am entirely willing to accept the responsibility for everything that has taken place. The Cabinet itself has ordered the deportations."

On another occasion, the ambassador was summoned to Talaat. In *Ambassador Morgenthau's Story* he quotes Talaat as saying:

> I have asked you to come today so that I can explain our position on the whole Armenian subject. We base our objections to the Armenians on three distinct grounds. In the first place, they have enriched themselves at the expense of the Turks. In the second place, they are determined to domineer over us and to establish a separate state. In the third place, they have openly encouraged our enemies. They have assisted the Russians in the Caucasus and our failure there is largely explained by their actions. We have, therefore, come to the irrevocable decision that we shall make them powerless before this war is ended.

Morgenthau continues:

On every one of these points I had plenty of arguments in
rebuttal. . . . Massacre as a means of destroying business
competition was certainly an original conception! His general
charge that the Armenians were "conspiring" against Turkey
and that they openly sympathized with Turkey's enemies merely
meant, when reduced to its original elements, that the Armenians were constantly appealing to the European Powers to protect
them against robbery, murder, and outrage. The Armenian
problem, like most race problems, was the result of centuries of
ill-treatment and injustice. . . . I argued for a long time along
these and similar lines.

"It is no use to argue," Talaat answered, "we have already
disposed of three-quarters of the Armenians; there are none at
all left in Bitlis, Van, and Erzerum. The hatred between the
Turks and the Armenians is now so intense that we have got to
finish with them. If we don't, they will plan their revenge."

Ambassador Morgenthau was not the only high official
working to call attention to the Armenian tragedy. In October, the former British ambassador to the United States,
Viscount Bryce, delivered an address in the House of Lords
that shook the normally unemotional assembly to the core.
He declared that virtually the whole Armenian nation had
been wiped out, and he doubted whether there was any case
in history of a crime "so hideous and on so large a scale."

"The death of these people," he said, "resulted from the
deliberate and premeditated policy of the gang now in posses-
sion of the Turkish Government. Orders for the massacres
came in every case directly from Constantinople. In some
instances local Governors, being humane, refused to carry out
the orders and at least two Governors were summarily dismissed for this reason."

Chapter 20

At the time that Viscount Bryce delivered this address to the House of Lords, Ramzi, only a few months away from graduation, still had not heard from Efronia. Half mad with worry, he could hardly bring himself to read the papers. How, he asked himself, would he get into Turkey once school was over? When would this war end? What concerned him above all was what he heard from Münever Hanem in Aintab. There had been a couple of letters with the most alarming news: Aintab Armenians had been deported, and Münever Hanem had heard nothing from Efronia.

Ramzi could hardly bring himself to look at her picture. What had those eyes seen? Could they see anything at all anymore?

One day, when Efronia was sitting in their small Aintab living room, trying to calm her thoughts by working on her lace tablecloth, Flora Hanem came to visit. She was the wife of the physician who cared for Münever Hanem and her family. When Ramzi had visited Aintab for those fifteen days before he returned to school, Efronia had gone to great pains to keep this doctor and his family out of the picture, so that news of her relation with Ramzi would not leak out into the Armenian community. Flora Hanem had never found out that Efronia knew Münever Hanem, and when she innocently brought up the family's name over a cup of coffee, Efronia's heart almost stopped.

"I went to visit the wife of one of my husband's patients the other day," said Flora Hanem. "Her name is Münever Hanem, and she is the wife of Osman Zade Midhad Bey. She is looking for someone to tutor her eight-year-old son. I told her about you and your little school, and she asked me to find out if you would be interested in giving Turkish lessons to her son. I hear he is a nice little boy."

A wild hope entered Efronia's heart. Here was a chance to get in touch with Ramzi's family again, perhaps even have some news from him. She struggled hard not to give Flora Hanem any indication that she knew Midhad Bey's family.

"Yes, I could teach the boy if they want me to," she said. "Why don't you bring them over here in a couple of days, so I can meet them."

A few days later, Münever Hanem, Flora Hanem, and the little boy appeared at the door. Münever Hanem and Efronia were introduced by Flora Hanem, and they pretended not to know each other. Throughout the brief visit, they discussed the practical details: what textbook to buy; what day the boy would start his lessons. When Münever Hanem left, she said she would be back the next day.

Efronia felt she had discovered a treasure:

Münever Hanem came back the next day with her maid to show her the way to my house. Münever now took me aside and gently kissed my cheeks. "How happy I am that you have not been deported," she said. *"I was certain that you, too, had been sent away with all the other Armenians. I was so terribly worried about you since I could not get any information about you. When I heard from Flora Hanem that you were still here, I was delighted."*

Then she broached the subject of Ramzi. "Are you getting any letters?" she asked.

"No," I said. "I was getting some earlier, but now it has been months since I have heard from him."

"I must write to Ramzi as soon as possible," Münever Hanem said. "It looks as though his letters are not reaching your hands."

She asked me a lot of questions and told me to write to Ramzi; her maid would then pick up my letter when she brought the boy over, and Münever Hanem would mail it along with hers.

She could only send her son three times a week since they lived far

*away and their carriage could not get through our narrow streets,
which meant that either she or her maid would have to bring him
personally. "My sister, I do not wish to renew your sorrow," she said
in parting. "But your mother took a bad step. The poor boy tried so
hard to take you with him because he knew, through his father, about
the calamities that were going to befall the Armenians."*

*Unable to restrain my tears, I said, "Dear sister, what could I
do? I was willing. No matter how much I begged my mother, she
would not consent. My poor mother now sees how unhappy I am and
how I suffer."*

*After Münever Hanem left, it was as if there was no strength left
in me. My sorrows were renewed. Yet at the same time I was very
happy to have received news of Ramzi. I was in no mood to busy
myself with the children. Many times, I tried to write that letter,
but I got nowhere. Finally, over several days, I wrote it and gave it
to Münever Hanem when she brought the boy.*

*We had now reached 1916. The war continued. However, al-
though the town criers were proclaiming news of Turkish victories
every day, it was clear that, instead of winning, the Turks were
getting weaker by the day and losing large territories.*

*Our lives were almost the same as they had been, but in the words
of a Turkish saying, "Should you suffer deprivation for forty days,
you get used to it." Our situation was like that. We were thankful to
God for not having been deported. My teaching the children turned
out to be a good way of keeping busy. We rarely saw our bride's face
except at mealtimes; otherwise, she sat by herself in her room. Down
the street, there were a couple of Armenian women whose husbands
were doctors who had been sent to the front. In the evenings, we
sometimes got together to play cards, and one of them started giving
me piano lessons. Time was passing. It was a monotonous life, but we
were happy to be alive.*

Later on, quite a few Armenian refugees began drifting back into

Aintab. All were women, and they were in the most pitiful condition. Many had lost their children and husbands. Their daughters had fallen into the hands of the gendarmes and were lost in the deserts. One woman told us that her two lovely daughters had thrown themselves into the Euphrates River instead of yielding to the bandits. Many came begging, but we could give them hardly anything, since we barely had enough to eat ourselves. They would empty the garbage cans and eat whatever they could find, be it clean or dirty. They were like living skeletons, these women. The tales they told! They would cry, and we would cry. Seeing them, we thanked God again that we had not been deported. Many of these women found work in Turkish and Armenian families. The ones we met were mostly from Constantinople and Sivas. They had been driven with the convoys to the desert and then found their way to our region, one by one. It was evident that many of them came from educated and well-off families.

Because my brother's wife was pregnant, she and Yacoub wanted to get one of these women as a maid to help her. The poor woman they chose was so happy. Although her looks had been spoiled by everything she had suffered, it was clear she had once been very beautiful. She loved us very much, and my mother took care of her like her own daughter.

A few months later, a great change came about in our family: our bride gave birth to a daughter. We were delighted. We called her Laura. She became a very happy occupation for us. As her own mother did almost nothing for her other than nursing her, we took on all of the baby's care. She was a very sweet child, and she grew up to be a very good-natured girl and woman, and remains so to this day.

A few weeks after I composed my letter to Ramzi and entrusted it to Münever Hanem's maid, I was overjoyed to receive a reply. Ramzi was immensely relieved to hear that I was still in Aintab, but he was full of worries and concerns for me.

I wrote back, begging him to be patient and telling him that God is great and we should rely on Him.

But we had scarcely had time to exchange a few letters when fate threw a new obstacle in our path. One evening, my cousin Dr. Hovsep came over to our house and asked to speak to my mother in private. He looked grave.

They said nothing openly, but I could see from my mother's face that there was a serious problem concerning me—some bad news.

My mother turned to me and said, "Get yourself ready, my dear. You are going to the doctor's house with him. You have been here, confined to the house, for so long and have been through so many difficulties that you must be quite tired of it by now. Dr. Hovsep wants you to go to their house and spend some time with his daughters. Alice is very ill, as you know, and she wants to see you."

I did not believe any of this, but I did not ask any questions. I got dressed, veiled my face, and left the house with my cousin. I noticed two soldiers waiting outside. Dr. Hovsep turned to me and said, "You walk with them. I will follow you."

We started walking. Dr. Hovsep lived some distance away. When we finally got there, the soldiers left, and I realized they were not real soldiers at all but two Armenian men who were dressed as soldiers to stop people from approaching us. It was dinnertime. None of us said anything as we ate.

The doctor's second daughter, Alice, had tuberculosis. Right next to the doctor's house, there was the empty house of a deported family. The doctor's family had made a door into that house from their own courtyard and placed Alice there because they were concerned that their younger daughters might get infected. Their oldest daughter had already died from tuberculosis a few years before.

They had me stay in one of the rooms off that courtyard, near Alice's room. That evening, I still had learned nothing about why Dr. Hovsep's family had brought me over. I could not sleep the whole night. In the morning we had breakfast together, and after we had eaten, the doctor's wife took me aside and finally explained the situation.

Two streets down from our house, there lived a Turkish family. They had a son, a municipal physician named Zeki Bey. It turned out he had been in love with me for a long time, and now he was determined to make me his wife. Until now, he had not had the courage to ask for my hand, but now that the Armenians were being persecuted, he was emboldened to make his move.

And if he could find no other way of making me his wife, he planned to abduct me.

Curtain

Efronia never found out how Dr. Hovsep had learned about Zeki Bey's intentions, but there is no doubt that her relatives took his threat very seriously. Their plan was for Efronia to spend some time in Dr. Hovsep's house, then to keep her out of harm's way.

Efronia told me the Zeki Bey story many times. As my understanding of Armenian grew, the details of the story came more sharply into focus: how the doctor's wife had told her never to open the outside door; how one day Zeki Bey's sister and mother had come to visit and she had barely had time to hide in the attic; how she passed two long months in that attic all by herself; how she spent time visiting the young Alice, whose life was ebbing. In this telling, there was a note of pride, a touch of vanity: this is how beautiful she had been. Too beautiful to be seen. It had been an adventure.

It was only later, when I realized what the backdrop to this story was, that I understood how real the threat to her freedom had been. Not only was she a highly desirable woman in the flower of her youth. She had also been an Armenian in wartime Ottoman Turkey, and as such, she had no other protection than that offered by those members of her family who— through luck or cunning—had been able to escape deportation.

But what I had never realized, until I read Efronia's story

and learned about Ramzi, was that the Zeki Bey episode may have contributed directly to the snapping of the fragile link that united her with the love of her life.

In her isolation in Dr. Hovsep's attic, Efronia got news from her family on a regular basis through Dr. Hovsep himself. Occasionally, Ovsannah, too, came to visit.

On one such occasion Ovsannah told Efronia: "Münever Hanem has been coming over to ask for you. She came twice within three days."

"Mother, what news did she bring? What did she say? What did you say about me?"

"I told her you had been very tired and that we had sent you to Aleppo to stay with a relative for a while, to get some rest."

It was a preposterous explanation, and on hearing it, Münever Hanem had seemed very upset and incredulous. How could Efronia's family possibly let her travel to Aleppo at a time like this? An Armenian girl traveling over roads lined with the corpses of deported Armenians and with Kurdish tribesmen and bandits lying in wait at every mountain pass? And what was she going to tell Ramzi now, who was begging for news about Efronia with increasing despair? Was he really going to believe that Efronia's family had sent her to Aleppo?

Given the circumstances, Münever Hanem seems to have concluded that Ovsannah could not be telling the truth. Something very serious must have happened to Efronia.

With a heavy heart, Münever Hanem went home to write a letter to Ramzi. And in her attic hideaway, Efronia spent countless hours worrying about what news of her Münever Hanem's letter to Ramzi in London might have contained. She describes her fears:

When my mother told me about Münever Hanem's visit to our house, the mere thought of what Ramzi would think when he heard from Münever Hanem made my head explode.

I decided that the next time my mother came, I would have some words with her. And when my mother came back, I opened up with tears: "Mother, don't you regret now that you didn't send me off with Ramzi? What kind of a life is this, Mother? Had I been sent to Deir Zor, I would have become food for hyenas or the wife of a bedouin. God saved me from that, but now we have to deal with Zeki Bey, who wants to abduct me. Let's see how I'm going to escape from his hands during these awful times! Don't you pity me now?"

A little later, the young Alice succumbed to tuberculosis. The family had a small, private ceremony, for no priest was available. Even the death of an Armenian had to be kept quiet. Nevertheless, for many days afterward, quite a few of the family's Turkish friends came to offer their condolences. Efronia hardly dared to leave her room.

One day, Dr. Hovsep came with good news: Zeki Bey was about to be transferred to another city. He was going to take his mother and sister along. A few more weeks passed, and the transfer was confirmed. Dr. Hovsep decided that Efronia could return home safely.

Back at home, Efronia lost no time getting in touch with Münever Hanem. It had been over four months since she had heard from Ramzi. She sent word that she was ready to resume her lessons with the boy.

When Münever Hanem finally came over, Efronia told her everything that had happened: how Zeki Bey's abduction plans had come to light and how she had spent all this time hidden in the attic.

Münever Hanem was immensely relieved to see her again and handed her two letters from Ramzi.

Efronia opened them immediately. Münever Hanem studied her face as she was reading, scanning the letters for news.

The news was not good: Ramzi had been ill. He had been in the hospital with acute appendicitis. He had had an operation, and his mother had come to be with him.

The letters were old. Münever's news was more recent: she reassured Efronia that Ramzi was fully recovered.

Efronia finished the letters after Münever Hanem had left. "I read them once, and then I read them over again, though I could not read them without getting upset and crying. Ramzi had written his thoughts about me when he was in the hospital; he had written about his dreams and about his longings."

What no one knew at the time was that Ramzi had written these letters through a haze. When he had his operation, the doctor had given him morphine for the pain. The drug, Ramzi found, offered him relief not only from his physical pain. Increasingly, he found that the only way he could bear to think about Efronia, and what might have happened to her, was through that soothing haze.

Ramzi was becoming addicted.

Meanwhile, Aintab suffered through one of the most severe winters on record, as Efronia describes:

The winter of that year—1917—was extremely cold. It snowed for weeks on end, and it became very difficult to heat the houses. Firewood and charcoal were hard to come by. The Turks were tearing down the vacant houses of deported Armenians and selling the window frames and doors for fuel.

In the middle of this cold spell, Dr. Hovsep's wife came down with pneumonia. She had long suffered stomach ailments and was already very thin. The room the family lived in was on the ground floor and very damp. Dr. Hovsep, fearing that his wife might come down with tuberculosis if she stayed in that room, wondered if she might move in with our family for a while.

This was my mother's chance to repay Dr. Hovsep for all the help he had given us. She took his wife in and gave her her own bedroom. For five weeks, while it snowed and snowed, we took care of the sick woman and managed to nurse her back to health.

Somehow, we got through that winter, but that didn't mean my troubles were over.

Until that February, the letters from Ramzi kept coming, full of worries, full of despair. But then they suddenly stopped. Initially, this did not worry me too much. These, after all, were not normal times. The letters were probably getting lost somewhere. The war was still on. There was heavy censorship.

Around that time, another strange thing happened. Though Münever Hanem's son kept coming to our house for his lessons, Münever Hanem herself stopped coming to see me. The boy was always brought to me by the coachman or the maid.

Finally, I began to worry. One day, I asked the maid why her mistress no longer brought the boy. The maid, looking startled, said Münever Hanem was very busy. Several more weeks passed, and it was the same: no Münever Hanem and no letters from Ramzi.

And the maid always said the same thing: her mistress was very busy. But this explanation no longer satisfied me.

Suspicions began to awaken in my mind: What could keep Münever Hanem so busy? After all, she had two maids. And if a letter had arrived for me from Ramzi, what reason could she have not to send it on to me?

A thousand and one possibilities crossed my mind. The next time the maid brought the boy, I took her aside and pleaded with her sweetly to reveal the truth.

"Don't be afraid to tell me what you know. I won't say anything to your mistress," I said.

"Dear miss, please don't force me. My mistress instructed me over

and over not to tell you why she isn't coming here, no matter how much you might try to make me do it. If I told you, she would scold me, and I would lose my job. I don't want to do that; they're a good family, and they pay me well. I will say only that my mistress spills her tears every day."

And now the maid, too, began to cry.

I gave up. It was impossible to make her talk. I felt even more confused than before. I wondered if there was some marital discord between Münever Hanem and her husband. Perhaps she had received some bad news from a close relative. Perhaps she was ill.

The day after our conversation, the maid did not show up with the boy. He was brought by the coachman, instead. I asked no further questions for fear that he, too, would give me the same answer as I had received from the maid and then tell his mistress about my questions. I was afraid that if that happened, Münever Hanem might stop sending the boy altogether, and then I would be deprived of all hope of hearing about Ramzi.

A few more weeks passed. Seemingly because I did not ask any further questions, the maid once again accompanied the boy. This time, I asked the girl only to tell her mistress that I missed her very much and wondered if she would bring the boy herself sometime so that I would have a chance to see her.

The next day, the maid brought back word that her mistress also longed to see me and that she would send her coachman to pick me up at my sister's house on Saturday. My sister was invited to come along.

When we arrived, Münever Hanem met us. She was dressed in black. Embracing me and clinging to me, she began crying. My cheeks became wet with her tears.

We sat down. She was silent. We were silent.

Finally I said, "Dear sister, why have you stayed away from us for so long? Have no letters come from Ramzi at all? I thought that if a letter had arrived, you would have sent it on to me with the *maid. Haven't you heard from him? I'm very worried. Has he fallen ill again?"*

She looked at me and began to cry again. "My dear sister," she said, "what shall I say? How shall my lips have the strength to tell you what has happened? The person so dear to us . . . and so dear to you . . ."

I cut her short and cried, "I beg you, tell me quickly: what has happened?"

She came and sat next to me. She took my hands in hers, and then she embraced me. We were both crying now. "Sister," she said. "Your Ramzi . . . Our beloved Ramzi . . . We have lost him forever, this precious, peerless boy. We have lost him in the flower of his youth. He has been the victim of an accident. One night, on his way home, he was in a serious car accident and injured his head. He lost consciousness and died in the hospital two days later. It was impossible to save him. They sent word to his parents. His mother and father went there to obtain permission to take his body to Persia and bury him in the family tomb. His parents, who were getting ready to go to his graduation . . . now they have gone to cry over his lifeless body."

I do not know what happened to me. It was as if lightning had struck. Everything turned dark around me. I could not speak. I tried to say something, and then I fainted.

22

Aftermath

"This is a very sad story," said Efronia one evening as she was watching *Romeo and Juliet* on television in California. And then, surprising me with the intensity of her look, she continued, "May God grant that you and your husband grow old on the same pillow and that you see your children and your grandchildren get married."

This was the year she was writing down her love story, but I didn't know it then. The blue binder with the Armenian curlicue letters lay open in front of her on the small table. She leaned over and closed it.

I wondered why her fingers were having so much trouble finding their way back into crocheting the tablecloth she was working on for her granddaughter, Nina. Now, reading her story, I understand.

When I opened my eyes, my sister and Münever Hanem were pouring cold water on my face and holding smelling salts in front of my nose. I still could not speak. Münever Hanem was caressing my face and stroking my hair.

We sat quietly for a while. The maid served coffee. I looked at the house and remembered the days we had passed here, Ramzi and I. I almost expected him to come out of one of the rooms, looking tall and handsome. But it was a dream, and it remained a dream. In reality,

*the world had turned dark for me. The sun had lost its light during
the day, and the moon had lost its light at night.*

*I shall not write any more about this. The reader can imagine the
rest. I simply cannot describe what it was like years ago when I fell
in love, when I was barely twenty years old. But I must confess that
when I wrote these lines, Ramzi's face was in front of me, and his
sweet words were in my ears, even after all these years.*

*Years later, I saw the story of Romeo and Juliet. I watched it
through my tears. It was just like our love—except that they were
fortunate enough to die together and to be buried together.*

Ramzi was gone. But like a restless spirit, he was going to
haunt Efronia's life in strange ways during those years after
the war.

As the survivors were returning and efforts got under way
to start rebuilding what was left of the Armenian communities, forces were already gathering that would eventually sweep
the remaining Armenians off their ancestral lands altogether.

By October 1918, the Ottoman Turkish armies were de-
feated; their resistance to the Allied powers had crumbled
everywhere. Turkey sued for peace, and the Armistice of
Mudros, which ended the war, was signed in November. The
three Young Turk leaders fled the country on board a German
vessel. None of them lived long after that: Enver was killed
during the subsequent fighting in Central Asia. Djemal was
assassinated by an Armenian in Tiflis. Talaat, who was living
in Berlin under an assumed name, was killed in broad daylight
by a young Armenian, Soghomon Tehlerian, who was later
acquitted by a German court on the grounds of temporary
insanity brought on by the murder of his family by the
Ottoman Turks. The trial made international headlines and
focused attention on the atrocities against the Armenians.
After the war, the intense disagreements between the Allied

powers over what was to be done with the Ottoman Empire came to the surface. The Greeks, the Italians, the British and the French, the Russians and the Americans all had different territorial views. The participants at the Paris Peace Conference waffled and wavered. President Wilson, who had great personal sympathy for the Armenian cause, declared in point twelve of his Fourteen Points that "the other nationalities which are now under Turkish rule should be assured an undoubted security of life and an absolutely unmolested opportunity for autonomous development"; and an independent Armenian Republic was born in 1918, with the whole-hearted support—at least in theory—of every Allied power. But the Armenians soon found out that no one was willing to back up the new republic with armed support. It fell to the communists in 1920.

The peace conference had begun with the best intentions. It had sent a commission to Anatolia and the Caucasus under U.S. Major General James Harbord to gather facts about the massacres of the Armenians. The commission's report on "this most colossal crime of all the ages" brought world sympathy for the "starving Armenians" to new heights. Turkey, in the words of U.S. Ambassador Morgenthau, had proven itself "unfit to govern." Even the chief Turkish representative at the peace conference, the Grand Vizir Damad Ferid Pasha, admitted that the Ottoman government had perpetrated "misdeeds which are such as to make the conscience of mankind shudder forever." The Armenians, it was generally agreed, needed to be protected by a mandatory power until they could get back on their feet again.

The question was, who was going to take on this responsibility? Initially, there was a strong sentiment in the U.S. for taking on this task. An American bishop working with Near East Relief, a U.S. agency set up specifically for postwar

Armenian aid, said: "These people look to the United States in their present appalling condition. They cry out for the United States." But even while the peace conference was in session, the isolationist sentiment in the United States was growing. The country was war-weary and wanted its boys to come home. Eventually, this sentiment led to the U.S. rejection not only of a mandate for the new Armenian state but even of U.S. membership in the League of Nations. After the war, splendid isolation looked increasingly good, and without the backing of the United States, Great Britain, France, and Italy began their own retreat from supporting the Armenian cause.

In Efronia's part of the country, the squabbles between the Allies in Paris did not go unnoticed by the Turks. Delays in the peace treaty provided just the time the nationalist Turkish movement under Mustafa Kemal needed to surface and organize. Before any peace treaty had been signed, the movement had gathered impressive strength under the charismatic Kemal—later known as Atatürk, or Father of Turkey. While the British and the French, in accordance with the armistice, halfheartedly occupied various "strategic points" in the interior, Kemal and his fledgling government in Ankara were organizing to free Turkey from all foreign troops.

One of the "strategic points" occupied by the Allies was Aintab.

There had been a news blackout in Aintab during much of the war, but nothing could prevent the news of the last battles between Turkish troops and the British forces under the command of General Allenby from reaching the town. When news came of the triumphant entry into Damascus of Arab troops under Emir Feisal and Colonel Lawrence, everyone knew this was the end of the Ottoman Empire.

A few months later, General Leslie's Nineteenth Brigade, which consisted of five regiments of Indian cavalry and a labor corps of six thousand Indian soldiers, occupied Marash, Aintab, and Urfa.

When the British neared Aintab, the Armenians rejoiced, Efronia among them. In particular, those refugees who had come from other towns and sought refuge in Aintab were glad they would be able to return home soon. There were no men or children among them—the men and children had been massacred or kidnapped.

The British began to move in with their troops. They surrounded the city and occupied all the government buildings. Their first task was to get rid of those government officials who had taken part in the deportation of the Armenians.

The American College was also occupied by the British, who converted its rooms to offices. And anyway, there were very few men of college age left. The same was true of the professors. The American professors had returned to America, and the four Armenian professors who had been deported had been killed. The seminary for women also did not open for similar reasons.

The devastated Armenian community was now trying to organize itself again. Some schools reopened, and the churches were trying to get on their feet, as Efronia describes:

The Protestants in Aintab had three churches. The Second Church, to which we belonged, had been converted by the Turks into a stable, and much of our congregation had been deported and lost. The furnishings of the church had been stolen, too, so we thought it best to join with the First Church. Although that building, too, had been damaged, and not a single one of its chairs and benches had been left

159

behind, the congregation repaired it fairly well, got together the necessary furnishings, and invited Reverend Bulbulian of Aleppo to be its pastor.

The elders of the church now had an idea: they wanted to form a joint choir, with members from the Protestant and the Apostolic churches, and to put on a concert to honor and to show their gratitude to the officers of the British occupying force. With some effort, they gathered enough young people to form the choir, which rehearsed intensely for a month. I was a member of this choir.

The British accepted the invitation cordially. The large hall of the Apostolic church was chosen as the most suitable location for the concert. Even though it had been sacked, the organizers spent quite a bit of money and got the necessary furnishings. That is where the concert took place, and the British guests appreciated it very much. We sang songs in English and Armenian, and they all came forth and congratulated us at the end.

Although for a brief time after the war the Turkish government took full responsibility for the massacre of the Armenians and even moved to punish the perpetrators, the political winds soon changed. Subsequent governments have all claimed that there was actually no planned massacre of the Armenians at all. There had only been a war; and in wars, as everyone knows, people suffer. Certainly, lots of Armenians had died in the process of "relocation." But lots of other people had died and suffered, too. What had happened was most unfortunate, but why dwell on the past? These were simply "erroneously interpreted tragedies," as the Turkish ambassador to the United States later put it. The Armenians had had to be moved, went the explanation, because they constituted a potential fifth column within the Ottoman Empire. But there had been no genocide. After all, nobody had ever counted the dead.

This genocide was only "alleged."

In some academic circles, it became a numbers game. Had one million perished, or was it two? Or was it only three hundred thousand?

A young California schoolteacher who had spent the summer traveling in Turkey once said to me: "It's too bad these people are getting such a bum rap for that Armenian stuff. Of course, people perished. They do in all wars. And anyway, it's soon eighty years ago, for God's sake. Why not just forget it?"

It is working, I thought. It is a powerful combination: historical revisionism, geopolitical realities, and the powerful pull of the Orwellian memory hole.

Efronia used to say, "We want so little. We don't want land or money. We just want our history back. We just want them to say that it happened. What are they afraid of? After all, it wasn't the present-day government that massacred the Armenians; it was the old one, the Ottomans."

The Minority Rights Group International in London put it somewhat differently:

> To anyone who has read the relevant literature, and who is not a dedicated Turkist, it is absurd that the "official doctrine" propagated in Ankara is that there never was an Armenian problem, or if there was, that it was just the problem either of a "civil war," an absurd idea, or of a few bandits and subversives who met their just deserts. Too many people are learning the truth for these views to have credence much longer. It would unquestionably be in Turkey's interest to recognize that a crime was committed against the Armenians in 1915; although no Turkish government has shown any moral courage in that direction.

The presence of the troops in Aintab was a welcome reprieve from the nightmare of the war. If Efronia heard people worrying about what would happen if the British left, she does not write about it.

She had something else to worry about: several new suitors were appearing on the scene. How, with Ramzi gone, would she now find a way to turn them down?

23

New Suitors

With the British Army stationed in Aintab, the Armenians were groping their way back to a normal life. But reminders of the catastrophe were everywhere: skeletal women with stories "almost impossible to listen to," as Efronia puts it, were rummaging through garbage, looking for something to eat. Some of them took shelter in partially destroyed houses that had belonged to Armenians. Others had joyful reunions with trusted Turkish friends with whom they had left their belongings before they were deported. And although most of the Turkish population took a dim view of the Armenians' happiness about the British occupation, people dared to hope that the nightmare of the war years was finally over.

One of the many Armenians who did not return to Aintab was the young doctor, Garabed, who had wanted so desperately to get engaged to Efronia before he went off to the war. She told me the story many years later in Beirut, and I remember feeling puzzled that Efronia did not seem terribly affected by this man's death. If anything, I now realize, it was a relief. She would not have to fight her way out of another marriage proposal. In her memoir, she makes it amply clear how she was feeling about the prospect of getting married to anyone:

As far as my own life was concerned, I had given up all hope for the future. I was in a state of confusion; I felt as if I lived in thin air. The world turned dark for me, and I had given up on life. Everything was bleak. Nothing gave me joy. After the death of my beloved, I turned my face from the world. Even if a king had asked for my hand, I would not have married him.

My brother Yervant had returned safe and sound, but with his prospects for the future as dim as ever. "Come on, sister," he used to say to me only half jokingly, "come on, marry a rich man and pay for my education!"

It was as if God heard my brother's voice. We learned that a young man by the name of Krikor had returned from America. He was a close relative of my brother-in-law's, and he had gone to America before the war and become very wealthy. Now he had come to Aintab to get married and then to return to America.

One day I came home from school and found my mother very preoccupied. I knew something important was on her mind. Not asking any questions, I went up to my room, where I changed my clothes and sorted out my students' papers on my desk. In a little while, my mother came up with two cups of coffee on a tray. "My dear, I waited for you to come down to drink your coffee before you settled down to work," she said.

I thanked her. We drank our coffee and talked about the events of the day. Then she turned to me and said, "My daughter, do you know who came for a visit today?"

"Who?"

"I think you remember him. He went to America before the war. He is a close relative of your brother-in-law's. He has changed his name in America. He was a very good-looking young man, and now he has become even more handsome and fashionable, even though he has put on a lot of weight. After you left for school this morning, he came to see me. I welcomed him and asked how his mother and father were doing. He said, 'Ovsannah Hanem, I have come to you for an important matter. I have a request. Even before I went to America, I had made up my mind to ask for the hand of your daughter Efronia,

but I was not in a position to do so. I then went to America, the war started, and I was obliged to remain there. When the war was over, I returned right away to reveal this wish to you. I hope you won't refuse me.' He told me quite a bit about his business; how very successful he has become, and so on."

"Fine," I immediately cut my mother short. "So how did you answer him?"

"I told him I could not give him an answer before I had had a chance to talk with you. I said you may or may not remember him, and he said he would come back on a day when you are here and that we could talk again. Meanwhile, he asked me to tell you about his visit and about his hopes and wishes."

When I heard this, it was as if lightning had fallen on my head. At first, I was speechless. Then I turned to my mother and said, "Dear mother, I do not want to hurt your feelings, but are we going to open up these old accounts again? Must I repeat over and over again all that I have already told you? My whole life and all my secrets are open to you. But I must tell you—for the last time—that I am not going to get married. There is going to be no wedding for me on the face of this earth. You must surely understand that after the death of my beloved Ramzi, whom I worshiped, there can be no other suitor for me—no matter how rich, no matter how handsome. There is no man on this earth who can replace him.

"And also, you should know that even though his death has permanently separated us from each other, it is you who separated us in the first place.

"If I have hurt your feelings, I beg your forgiveness. My life means nothing to me anymore. The pleasures of the world no longer interest me. Just as he died like an angel without fulfilling his wish, so shall I. From now on, I have decided to dedicate my life to the care of the poor and the sick. I beg you, my dear mother, if you love me and do not want to torment me, no matter who comes to ask for my hand, *from now on, refuse him and do not even tell me about it. Please take pity on me for all I have suffered during these years."*

My poor mother left the room without a word. It was already dark. I took the locket with our pictures that Ramzi had given me and the handkerchief with which he had wiped my tears when we separated. I knelt down and, in tears, begged God to help me. I did not go downstairs, and after a while, my mother brought dinner up to my room. We said nothing to each other, and she went down again.

Since the following day was a Saturday, I had no school, and I did not get out of bed. My mother brought me breakfast and sat down next to me. I could sense she was troubled. With a mother's love, she caressed my cheeks and implored me to listen to her.

"My dear, I know you do not want to listen to these things any longer," she said. "But as your mother, I have certain responsibilities. So please listen to the advice of your mother, who always thinks of you and your future. Please, my dear, you must give up these ideas. It is time now for you to get married, and you must consent to marry some suitable young man. You are now mature enough to think and decide. My dear, who will you rely on to care for you? You have no father, and we have no money. Your older brother has turned his face away from us. Your other brother is in dire need himself. The poor man is working day and night to set aside some money to go to school for at least one year. After that, he will return to work, and then he will try to finish school. How are you going to support yourself? If you remain firm in this decision, then how are you and how am I and how is your grandmother going to live? Take pity on yourself, and on us, and get married. All your suitors are rich and well established. None of them are men to be scorned or turned away."

I could contain myself no longer. I said, "I beg you, Mother, take pity on me. This is enough. You are pouring fire over my wounds."

My mother saw the condition I was in, and without saying another word, she got up, left the room, and closed the door.

I stayed in bed for the rest of the day, lost in dreams and heavy *thoughts. My life over the last few years passed like a caravan before my eyes. The best years of my youth had been spent in the midst of war, family turmoil, and my own sorrows. My future looked bleak. But I realized these thoughts would make me feel even more hopeless. I struggled to gain control of myself and to begin work on my future plans right away.*

Settling the Krikor affair, however, turned out to be very difficult. My mother finally had to tell him openly, "Don't come to see me anymore, please. There is nothing I can do. Go and see my daughter, and if you can convince her to marry you, do so."

Prompted by my mother's words, the young man started to visit us, unannounced, at times when he knew I would be at home. I turned him down repeatedly, but he would not give up hope. The last time he came to see me, he begged me to listen to him and to think his proposal of marriage over. He promised to make me happy in every way possible. He revealed to me the sincere love that he had had for me for several years. Let me only say that it all went in one ear and out the other. Finally, I tried to make him understand that there could be no marriage with a one-sided love, and I apologized for not being able to love him.

This time, he left without saying goodbye. He never came back. Later, we heard he was engaged to the daughter of a wealthy family and that they planned to get married right away and leave for America.

Since I was certain that other marriage proposals were going to follow, I thought it best to make my plans as soon as possible. That way, I would have a tangible excuse for refusing my suitors.

Efronia proceeded with the first part of her plan for the future by applying for admission to nursing school.

Two of her friends were nurses. They had left for college in Beirut during the first year of the war, while the roads were still open, and then they had found it impossible to return to

Aintab. This had proven a blessing in disguise: not only did they escape possible deportation, but since their parents could not send them money for their tuition, the nursing school had allowed them to stay on and study for free. The only condition was that they return to Aintab after the war and work at the local hospital until they had paid off their debts.

That is what they were doing when Efronia went to see them. She spoke with them at length about her hopes for college. They promised to inquire on her behalf, and Efronia went home with the address of the nursing school of the Syrian Protestant College of Beirut. She composed a letter in which she begged the school to accept her as a student. She would do whatever was necessary in return.

While Efronia was waiting for a reply, more marriage offers were coming in. "It would be superfluous to write more about them," she asserts. "The same story, the same problems. The worst part was that my repeated refusals created a great deal of discord in our family. We had arguments. My brothers began to exert more and more pressure. They also began to inquire into the reasons for my behavior."

Yervant, especially, kept probing. Why was his sister constantly turning people down?

"What reasons do I need?" Efronia asked. "Marriage doesn't interest me. I want to go to school and become more educated. I wanted to go to Marash College even before the war, but I couldn't."

Yervant thought all this was nonsense. What were her true reasons?

Efronia said nothing.

Yervant insisted: "You can't fool me. Surely you must have some serious reason. I suspect you love someone and are keeping it from us. Why can't you tell me the truth? If you love someone, and if he loves you and wants to marry you, then let him come here, so we can see him and get to know him. And if he is someone suitable, we'll get you engaged and married to him."

Efronia was no fool. She realized right away that her mother had prodded Yervant to make these inquiries. From now on, there was no more evading the truth. Yervant demanded an answer.

She embraced her brother and said, "Please don't torment me any more. I'll tell you everything . . . Yes, I loved someone . . . I wanted to marry him, but my mother would not consent."

"Fine," said Yervant. "So where is he now? Tell me, and I'll help you."

This was the moment she had been dreading. She drew a deep breath: "He is not alive; he died most painfully. But although he died, and more than a year has passed, his love is still in my heart. I cannot forget him. We had promised each other that only death would separate us. His death did separate us—but I am going to stand firm on my promise. I won't get married to anyone else. I am going to remain faithful to him. There is no one like him. He is an angel."

She got up and brought the locket with her and Ramzi's pictures in it and showed it to Yervant. "Tell me, brother, tell me the truth—how can anyone replace this peerless young man? It is impossible. I beg you to leave me to my sorrow . . ."

Breaking into tears, she told Yervant she could not continue. Very moved, he took her hands, and then he embraced her.

From that moment on, Yervant treated her differently, even to the point of helping to keep the suitors at bay.

A few days later, over coffee at the Aintab Armenian Educational Club, Efronia told her brother the whole story of Ramzi.

Yervant listened carefully and said: "My sister, I have listened to you, and I understand your sorrows. You are quite right in every respect. But the past is past. Everything would have been possible if he had been alive. Let me only say that our mother made a serious mistake in keeping all of this secret from us. She should at least have told me about it. Nonetheless, I must tell you, dear sister, that even though you were bound together by a sincere love, the fact that this young man did not belong to this community was a serious obstacle. It would not have been a suitable marriage. The entire Armenian community would have blamed us, and we would have been 'chewed up' in every mouth.

"Look, my dear, I realize he was worthy to be loved in every way. And I am very sorry he had to die in such an unfortunate accident. Even though I have never met him, just looking at his picture has awakened sympathy toward him in my heart. May God illuminate his soul.

"So do not forget him—keep his memory in your heart. But much time has passed now. You fulfilled your promise: you have not married anyone else until his death. You are wasting your life. I am sure that if he could know in his grave what course you have taken, he would not approve. He would not want your love for him to stifle your heart. Listen to the words of your loving brother who now knows your secrets and whose heart is one with you. It is a pity. You are young. Marry someone suitable whom you can love and whom you can be happy with."

After unburdening herself to her brother, Efronia felt a great relief. "There was a lightness in my heart," she writes. But that lightness did not last long before another suitor appeared on the horizon.

This one, she knew, would not be easy to get rid of. He

was a relative of Efronia's sister-in-law, Yester. And Yester, even under the best conditions, was a problem.

Yester never spent much time with Efronia and her mother. Their relationship had always been strained, and after a while Efronia's older brother, Yacoub, had moved out of the family compound with his family. But suddenly, there was an invitation to his house for dinner. When Efronia's family arrived, they found not only Yacoub and his family but another family as well: Yester's uncle, his wife, and their three grown children.

This family had gone to Jerusalem before the war, and from there they sent their oldest boy, Levon, to study dentistry in Paris. He had recently graduated. He was a handsome man, tall, blonde, with blue eyes, and, in Efronia's words, "unusually well dressed." And that whole evening, he would not take his eyes off Efronia.

She feared the worst.

Two days later, the family announced that they wanted to visit Ovsannah and her family. And now it was Yervant who came to the rescue.

"Don't invite them," he told Ovsannah. "Let's just leave my sister in peace for a while."

Ovsannah would have none of it. How could he be so sure that Efronia was the reason they wanted to visit? And, besides, how could they turn down a relative of their own bride?

The family came, and sure enough, they proposed. Ovsannah and Yervant had agreed in advance about how to respond.

"You are welcome, a thousand times welcome," Ovsannah said. "But we cannot give you an answer right away. We have only just gotten to know you. And to tell you the truth, my daughter has decided to go to Beirut for further study. She has applied and been accepted, and she is planning to leave toward the end of the summer."

Ovsannah was lying. The truth was that Efronia had just heard from Beirut. In order to accept her, the college would need her first year's tuition in advance. Twenty gold pieces. Efronia figured that, by the end of the year, she could save five gold pieces at the very most, since she had to help with the household expenses.

Nursing school was impossible.

The matter of the young dentist lasted for months. He just wouldn't give up. Efronia's repeated refusals exasperated her family and baffled her girlfriends.

Though he finally disappeared from her life, Efronia had had enough of suitors. She turned to her second plan. She decided to become a nun.

24

Aram

With the strong determination that characterized Efronia's every action well into her ripe old age, she now acted on her plan to become a nun. So far, the world had been a vale of tears for her. She was ready to turn her back on it for life.

She knew a family whose daughter was a nun, and she visited them one afternoon. The nun happened to be at home as well. After Efronia explained the purpose of her visit, the women looked at her in stunned silence. Why on earth was this beautiful young Protestant girl thinking of taking the veil? The nun stared at her, incredulous. She said, "I must warn you: a nun's life is not easy."

Nevertheless, she told Efronia that she would make an appointment for her with the mother superior.

Efronia went home to wait. The next two weeks passed very slowly, but somehow, with the convent at the back of her mind, the ardors of the current suitor were easier for her to bear. Soon, she told herself, there would be an insurmountable wall between herself and all the flowers, the presents, and the promises of eternal love that she was being showered with. All she wanted was to live in peace with her memories of Ramzi in the silence behind that wall.

One afternoon, there was a message for her: the nun was ready to take her to the mother superior. On her way to the convent that afternoon, Efronia silently rehearsed what she was going to say, and she felt a wild hope growing in her heart.

The mother superior received her with a friendly smile. So, Miss Nazarian wanted to become a nun? In order to determine her suitability, she explained, she needed to hear Miss Nazarian's reasons for wanting to enter a convent.

Efronia felt compelled to tell the truth. She gave a brief account of her engagement to Ramzi and its tragic end. As she was speaking, she must have sensed her chances dwindling; she ended her little talk in tears by begging the mother superior not to turn her down.

There was a moment of silence. The mother superior looked Efronia deep in the eyes and very slowly shook her head: "I am very sorry, my daughter, but I cannot help you. I do not see you becoming a nun; it would not be the right thing for you. You will not be able to sacrifice your life for this goal; yours are not the right reasons. Besides, my daughter, an attractive girl like you cannot become a nun. We have tried this before, and it only results in endless headaches. The girls want to leave before one year is up, and the young men who are after them never leave us in peace. I am sorry, but believe me, this is not for you."

Efronia looked at her and insisted: "Dear Mother, I have confessed to you that my beloved is dead. I can assure you there will be no one to bother you. I will . . ."

The mother superior cut her short. "That is all, my daughter. I wish you well."

Alone in her room later that evening, Efronia sat motionless with her head in her hands for a long time. In the silence, she was hearing the doors to her future closing, one after another. Or so she thought.

Some time before all this, while the war had still been going on and while the letters from Ramzi were still coming from London, Yacoub sent word home to his mother and his sister that he was bringing someone home for dinner.

Yacoub did not say who was coming, but neither did he alert Efronia to keep out of the way, so they concluded that the dinner guest was not likely to be a Turk. That afternoon, they prepared a nice meal. "Eggplant *doghrama* and pilaf," Efronia notes seventy years later.

"In the evening, a respectable young man showed up," she adds. "I remembered him from Iskenderun. He was Aram Katchadourian, the younger brother of my cousin Marie's husband."

This was the same young man who had attracted Efronia's attention in Iskenderun by ignoring her during her family's occasional visits to his family. Aram had been polite and correct, but he had shown little interest in the fact that a young, attractive girl was present. Work was what seemed to interest him then, and that, it turned out, was what he had come for now.

After dinner, Yacoub and Aram retreated upstairs for a few hours. They couldn't finish all they had to do in one evening, and Aram returned several times during the following days to work out the details of a business deal with Yacoub.

One may wonder why Aram would have wanted to have anything to do with Yacoub after his family's disastrous experience with him in Iskenderun. Actually, Yacoub's dealings had been with Aram's two older brothers. Moreover, Yacoub had settled down considerably since then. And, after all, the two families were related by marriage—much would be forgiven between them. Last but not least, Aram by now was clearly interested in Efronia and befriending her older brother would have made good sense from his perspective.

Aram was already well-known in the Armenian community as an intelligent businessman with creative ideas and a keen nose for fresh opportunities.

Early in the war, he had made a most unusual deal.

Aram had made a shrewd observation: having noticed that the Turkish army had trouble provisioning its troops on a regular basis and that their food and ammunition carts kept breaking down on the difficult terrain, Aram quickly figured out an alternative provisioning plan. He made some calculations, and when he was ready, he traveled to Aleppo and approached the military governor there.

"You give me as many exemptions from military service as you now have for men working to supply the troops, and I will provide a fail-safe method of getting the materiel and the food to your forces," he said.

Apparently, Aram struck the governor as a clever man, and the official decided to gamble. He issued sixty exemptions, and Aram said it was a deal.

When Aram returned to Aintab, he went out and bought a herd of camels and some mules. The animals were perfect for the terrain: they could take heavy loads, and they were sure not to break down. In addition, a caravan of camels needed only a few men to lead it.

And here lay the beauty of Aram's plan: he needed only a handful of men to do the actual work. He gave some of the exemptions to relatives and sold the rest for twenty-five gold coins each. That spring, a number of Armenian men in the Aintab area bought salvation from deportation for themselves and their families from Aram.

And not only did Aram himself manage to survive by virtue of this commission: the protection extended to his family as well, since they were connected to a person hired by the military.

This exhibition of business acumen in the lion's den earned Aram the respect and admiration of the Armenian community for years to come. It also made him a wealthy man.

Efronia, however, remained unimpressed by Aram when he came to work with Yacoub.

"I found him to be the same unemotional young man I had known in Iskenderun," she writes. "I am sure it never crossed my mind that I would one day become his wife. He was not the sort of man I dreamed of marrying. At any rate, there was no room for love in my heart for anyone other than Ramzi."

Two years had now passed since that visit. The war was over, Ramzi was dead, and Efronia had been turned down by both the nursing school and the convent. She was twenty-five years old.

In Aintab, there were rumors that the British would be withdrawing and French forces would be replacing them. People were openly worried about a possible confrontation between the Europeans and the Turkish nationalist forces that seemed to be getting stronger and better organized by the day.

One evening, when the Nazarians were having dinner, Ovsannah told her family that she had heard that Aram and his younger brother were in town. "People say they are both looking for wives."

Aram's younger brother got engaged first. As relatives of his sister-in-law Marie, Efronia and her family were invited to the engagement party.

Soon after that occasion, Marie came for a visit. She told Efronia about the efforts of one of her acquaintances to marry her daughter off to Aram.

"But," said Marie, "I don't think she'll succeed. I am sure that Aram will get the girl he has set his mind on."

Efronia writes: "Neither my mother nor I said anything, and we didn't ask who that girl might be. But I had the presentiment that I was the one he had decided on.

"Fear entered my heart."

Efronia did not have to wait long to find out her presentiment had been correct. One evening, Aram and his sister-in-law Marie (Aram's own parents were no longer alive) announced their intention to come for a visit.

"One didn't have to be a prophet," says Efronia, "to know they were coming to ask for my hand."

When they arrived, Efronia was there to offer everybody coffee, but as soon as she did so, she left the room and went downstairs.

This passage from the memoir begins with Efronia's mother's reply to the marriage offer, which Efronia remembers as a model of tact and diplomacy:

"Your visit is most welcome," my mother said, "but I cannot give you an answer now. You are no strangers to us. Both we and my daughter know you well, so it will not take her long to form an opinion. Unfortunately, I must forewarn you that there have been quite a few suitors, and there is no lack of them right now, but she has refused each of them and continues to refuse everyone. She claims she does not yet wish to get married. Instead, she wants to pursue her education for a few more years. She wanted to go to Marash College but was not able to because of the war. Nonetheless, please give us some time to think this proposal over, and I will let you know."

My mother called me upstairs. I had already prepared the refreshments for our guests. They enjoyed our hospitality for a while.

After they left, my brother Yacoub stayed behind to talk to me. His opening words were harsh. Quite rudely, he turned to me and said, "Let me see you refuse this one also! Come to your senses! We

*cannot refuse someone like Aram, and you are not going to reject him.
Speak up right away and give us your consent."*

I lowered my head and made no reply.

*My mother understood the difficulty I was in. She turned to my
brother and said, "Marriages are not to be forced. We pressured your
oldest sister, and she became unhappy and remains so to this day.
Give Efronia time; let her think about it."*

My brother got up and left, muttering to himself.

Perhaps Aram succeeded where all the others had failed
because he would not play by the rules. He refused to wait for
the deliberations. The next day, he appeared at the Nazarians'
doorstep, unannounced, and asked if he could speak to Efronia
in private.

Efronia remembered the occasion well:

*"Look, Efronia," Aram told me, "although I came here last night
with my sister-in-law, I did so only for the sake of civility. I don't
need intermediaries. This is a matter that concerns you and me. It is
we who must agree with each other. It is we who will love each other.
It is we who will get married and form our family.*

*"I have long admired you and liked you. When you came to
Iskenderun, I heard that you had many suitors, all of whom you
turned down. At that time, however, I expressed no interest and made
no offers. I was not too young, but I was not prepared to marry. I
still worked for my brothers. I wanted to attain a certain position
before I married. But the war intervened. And although you probably
know all this, let me tell you briefly my own and my family's
circumstances during the four years of the war.*

*"Since Iskenderun was a seaport, it was shelled very heavily from
the start of the war. The people fled, and we, too, were obliged to
send our families to Aintab. We made a serious mistake by not
sending them to Cyprus. During the deportations from Aintab, my*

family managed to escape to Aleppo. I myself stayed in Iskenderun. I sold everything we had and placed the money in a bank, thinking it would be safe there. We had a lot of wealth. Our stores were full of goods, and my two brothers' houses were full of valuables. I took along only a thousand gold pieces and went to Aleppo thinking that the war would not last long and that we would soon return. I was badly mistaken.

"When I arrived in Aleppo, I found that the money my brothers had taken with them was almost gone. They had large families, and life was very expensive. When I saw their situation, I immediately got down to work and obtained the commission to provision the regional army. Without fear, I went to Marash and Islahiyeh. I think you know about my life and work at the time. I worked hard and made a great deal of money. Your brother Yacoub, who helped me with this project, profited from this work.

"As you know, my brother is here, and he is engaged to be married soon. My sister became engaged in Kilis, and she, too, will be getting married. Although I have given them their share of my earnings, I have nonetheless taken on all their wedding expenses. And now that I have discharged my obligation, I decided that I, too, should get married.

"As I confessed, I chose you. And I must also confess that I love you most sincerely, and I beg you not to refuse me. Trust me: I am prepared to love you, to respect you, and to devote my life to making you happy."

He expressed himself with such affection and sincerity that I admired his sweet words and intelligent thoughts.

Before he left, he turned to me and said, "If you have any questions, don't hesitate to ask me, and I will answer them."

I fell into deep thought. My hopes lay shattered on all sides. My brother Yervant was leaving for the university in Beirut in September. I would be left with my mother and my grandmother. The political situation was getting worse. We feared that fighting would break out between the European forces occupying Aintab and the Turks.

I wondered what would happen to me if this war broke out. If the schools did not reopen, if I could not teach, how would we live? That became my biggest concern. And if war broke out again, what would be the fate of the Armenians? The prospect of more massacres horrified me.

I decided to talk things over with my brother Yervant. He was already aware of all my secrets. I felt like a bird with broken wings. I needed help to fly.

25

An Apple for Efronia

Efronia did not bring many things along with her when she fled Beirut for California in 1976; after all, she, now in her eighties, and Lucine, in her sixties, counted on returning in just a few months, when they assumed the civil war in Lebanon would have ended.

That made it even more remarkable that she had thought of packing the dried-up apple.

Though she had told me the apple story in Beirut, I had never seen the actual apple. But through repeated tellings, the apple had grown in my imagination, until it became a glossy sphere of purple and green. It wasn't until a few months after Efronia had passed away that I came across it. In an old chocolate box, wrapped in yellowed tissue paper and next to the announcement of Aram and Efronia's engagement party on July 17, 1919, was a small, brownish, shriveled object, a couple of inches in diameter. It took me a few moments to realize that this must have been Efronia's engagement apple.

I wished I could have seen it in its ripe and fragrant glory. Efronia's engagement party, a magnificent affair, had taken place soon after her talk with Yervant:

When Yervant came home in the evening, we had dinner and then we went upstairs. I told him about Aram's visit, including his proposal and the other things he had said. My brother listened to me in silence and then he asked, "Well, sister, tell me—what sort of impression did he make on you? Answer me truthfully."

"Brother," I said, "I can honestly tell you that I was favorably impressed by him. I became convinced that he is wise in his thoughts and sincere in his expression of love towards me and in his wish to marry me. He did not try to sway me with empty words.

"But there is still a struggle in my heart. Will I be able to love him? Will I be able to marry him? Will I be able to forget my old dreams? Will I be able to reconcile myself to what has happened, or will I keep remembering the past and make myself—and him— unhappy?"

I could not go on. I started to cry, and my mind stopped functioning.

My brother saw how I felt and came to my aid. "My dear sister, I understand you very well. You are quite right. But I ask you, I beg you, to set aside your old memories and dreams. You are intelligent; try to forget. In due time, you will love this worthy man. You have to think about yourself. You have suffered enough. You must think about whom you can live with happily, whom you can live with comfortably.

"You were quite wise not to have been duped by the other suitors. You were not taken in by their handsomeness or how madly in love with you they were. Good looks and wealth are transient, but the intelligent and worthwhile person remains worthwhile even if he loses all he has. My dear sister, have no fears, I am sure you will not regret marrying him."

My brother spoke so sweetly, so sincerely, and so well that I said, "My dear brother, I will spare no effort; I will conquer all my difficulties. Yes, I promise you to accept his offer."

My brother embraced me and said, "Thank you, dear sister. Your decision is going to solve your problems, and ours as well. I will send word to him tomorrow to come here so that you can tell him you have accepted his proposal."

It was as if a big burden had been lifted off my shoulders. I went to bed. I took out Ramzi's locket, and held it in my hands. I knelt down and asked God to help me not regret my decision and to ordain the best. I looked at Ramzi's photograph and kissed it in tears. I begged his forgiveness, and I promised him that his memory would remain forever in my heart.

Two years had passed since his death.

It was then the custom in Aintab that the final consent for a marriage should be obtained from the head of the bride's family. Thus, we decided to invite my brother Yacoub and his wife, my sisters and their husbands. We also invited my uncle Movses, who was the only surviving brother of my father and the oldest member of our extended family. He came accompanied by his wife and daughters.

Several relatives also arrived from Aram's side, and when they were all gathered at our house, my cousin Marie, who was married to Aram's brother, opened the subject by turning to my uncle: "We have come over tonight to ask for the hand of Efronia for my brother-in-law Aram. What do you say? We hope you will not refuse us."

She had barely finished her sentence, when my uncle interrupted her and said: "I will give him not only Efronia but my four daughters, as well. Aram has only one fault—he doesn't drink arak!"

Everybody laughed. Aram told him, "I promise I'll drink whenever I am with you."

During these ritual conversations, the prospective bride would not be present. When the discussion was over, my sister came to take me in to the two families. It was the custom that on the day that "the words were tied," the man's side would bring red apples as a congratulatory gift. Apples were very hard to find in Aintab. The village where one could find them was two hours away. Now the apples were brought in on a large tray. Aram gave me one, and I put this apple in my drawer, where it gradually dried up without rotting.

Chapter 25

Years later, when I came to California, I brought it along in a chocolate box with some of my other belongings, and it is still with me.

A day after it was agreed that I would marry him, Aram and his two sisters-in-law, as well as my brother and his wife, came to lunch to decide on the day of our engagement party. There were many arrangements to be made. We had to decide whom to invite, where to hold the party, and who was going to officiate, since Aram came from an Armenian Apostolic family and my family was Protestant.

The party was set for July 17 at Aram's grandfather's old house, which had been sold to another family we knew. It was a large house with a lovely courtyard and a fountain. My brother Yacoub took it upon himself to see these owners and obtain their consent. Then Aram came up with a surprise proposal. "Under these circumstances," he said, "each side should be given its due. I want the engagement to belong to you; so a Protestant minister should officiate and place the rings on our fingers. The wedding will be ours, and the archbishop and his priests will marry us. Furthermore, I will pay for all the expenses of the engagement, but I will leave the arrangements to you."

My brothers immediately got to work. They had to hurry because Aram had very little time before he had to return to Aleppo to attend to urgent business. They went to ask the owners of the old house, who cordially agreed to lend us the house for the engagement party. A dress was ordered for me—it was made of pink silk and was very beautiful. Word was sent to the Protestant church, and the Reverend Bulbulian gladly agreed to officiate. My family also asked the church choir to sing a few songs at the ceremony.

On the day of my engagement party, my brother Yervant did not go to work. He busied himself with all the remaining details. Aintab had no electricity at the time, and kerosene lamps were used for illumination. For this occasion, numerous lanterns were strung up. We had invited one hundred and fifty guests, so we had to rent many

186

chairs. Aram sent cases full of sweets, candies, and nuts; he also hired two waiters.

At seven o'clock the guests arrived. An organ had been brought over, and two violinists played as well. It was a very lovely engagement party, and everything worked out perfectly. The Reverend Bulbulian spoke very well. The choir sang three or four songs, including a sharagan, *a liturgical hymn, which they performed while we were exchanging the rings. The minister took the Bible, gave it to us and said, "Dear ones, let this book guide you in your life."*

The guests were all in a good mood—they ate, drank, and danced late into the night.

In the next days, many of our relatives invited us for dinner. Aram, in turn, offered two large banquets. One was for our relatives, and it was held at the picnic site of Kavaklik, the park by the stream. He hired a special cook who prepared all the food on the spot. The cook and his assistants slaughtered two sheep and made the meat into various kinds of kebabs. There were also many other dishes. We had both lunch and dinner at Kavaklik with some fifty to sixty people. The other banquet was on the occasion of Aram's brother Haroutune's wedding.

Aram stayed in Aintab for only fifteen days following our engagement. He could not stay any longer since he had business to attend to and arrangements to make for our wedding, which was to be held in Aleppo. But during those fifteen days, we were together virtually all the time.

Fifteen days. The same number of days that Ramzi had spent with Efronia before he returned to London in the time just before the war broke out. How that number must have triggered memories in Efronia's mind as she whirled through the many social engagements in connection with her betrothal. While she was thanking Aram for the jewelry he had ordered for her—the gold chains from Aleppo, the diamonds from Constantinople—did she wonder what these festivities would have been like if Ramzi had been the groom instead of Aram?

"I took everything for granted and did not derive much pleasure from it all," she writes.

And just in case she was forgetting Ramzi, fate arranged to play a special trick at the very end of Aram's stay in Aintab.

On the day of Aram's departure for Aleppo, he arrived early in the morning at Efronia's house with two carriages. One was his for the journey to Aleppo; the other was for Efronia and a young relative, Jemileh, who were going to accompany him to a point just outside the city and then return to Aintab.

As they set out from Aintab on the road through Kilis to Aleppo, Efronia suddenly realized that they were going toward Beshgüz, where she had said goodbye to Ramzi for the last time four years earlier.

Beshgüz. The white handkerchief waving from the carriage in the cloud of dust. Goodbye, my angel. Will I ever see you again?

When they got there, Aram, as if he were following a script written by an infernal stage master, suggested a cup of coffee in the coffeehouse by the road. There was only one in Beshgüz, and it hadn't changed. Efronia held her emotions in until she parted from Aram. But when she and Jemileh started their journey home, she could no longer restrain her tears. She writes:

Jemileh laughed at me and said, "You are crying because your fiancé went away. Shame on you! What is there to cry about? Very soon, you will be reunited with him."

I cried all the way back to Aintab.

Soon after he and his family left, I received a letter from Aram. They had had a comfortable journey, and everyone was well. His brother Sarkis sent his greetings and asked that our wedding not be delayed too long since he was planning to take his family and move back to Iskenderun. They wanted to leave before the weather turned cold. Aram asked if November 7 would be a convenient date for us, and I said it would.

Now that our wedding date was set, my family began to get organized. First, we had to prepare a trousseau, at least the essentials. We needed money. I had barely saved five gold pieces. My brother Yervant could not help; he was working day and night to save enough for his tuition for at least one year.

We pondered the matter at some length. Yervant had told our brother Yacoub that he should help a bit, but Yacoub had said that he could not. We thought of borrowing money, but from whom? My brothers-in-law were not the helping sort. We thought of selling my share in our house; the most suitable buyer would be my older brother Yacoub, should he accept the offer. We called him over, and my mother had a lengthy conversation with him. Finally, he accepted, buying my share in the house for fifteen gold pieces.

With the money in hand, we immediately set to work. I should mention that before he left, Aram had offered to give us whatever money we would need. But my mother refused, since it would have been embarrassing to accept money from him when she had a son who was a pharmacist. Aram asked us not to trouble ourselves with a large trousseau and said he would be sending quite a few things himself from Aleppo.

We were not in a position to prepare a large trousseau, anyway, but aunt Mennoush and my sister Aroussiak were very helpful to us. Auntie Mennoush had been an accomplished seamstress, and her sister, who had come up from Kilis, was similarly handy with needle and thread. For the next fifteen days, both of them would come in the morning and leave in the evening, and sometimes when it got late,

189

they would sleep over. Over those two weeks, almost all of my
trousseau was made.

    Aram had sent enough fabric from Aleppo for several formal
dresses, and this we gave to a seamstress. My measurements were sent
to Aleppo, and an additional four fine dresses made there now
arrived, along with my wedding gown. The gown was magnificent,
and everyone admired it. And there were many other presents: shoes,
handbags, perfumes, and very beautiful gold jewelery.

After the matter of the trousseau was settled, there were
other things to arrange. The first one was the question of
Ovsannah and Trvandah: after Efronia's wedding, where would
her mother and grandmother live? After much discussion,
they decided that Ovsannah would move with Yervant to
Beirut, and Trvandah would stay with Efronia's sister Azniv.

    That decided, Yacoub came with a proposition: he wanted
Efronia to move in with him and his wife for the few
remaining days, Efronia writes, "so that I would leave as a
bride from their house." This carried much symbolic significance. Ordinarily, a bride would leave for church from her
parental home. But if, like Efronia, she had lost her father,
she would sometimes leave from the home of a family who had
looked after her or acted as her benefactor.

    Yacoub now wanted this honor. Ovsannah promised to talk
to Efronia. But by this time, Efronia had had it with her
brother. "All my life," she writes, "I have tried to be
agreeable. In all matters, easy or difficult, I have tried to look
at the positive side of things. But it was impossible for me to
accept this offer from my brother and his wife. We had lived
with them for four years, and we had suffered through so
much at their hands, in silence. We had had to live on

Yervant's earnings and without any help from them. They did not worry about us for one single day, nor did they take any interest in us. When I became engaged, there was no money for a trousseau, yet my brother Yacoub never once asked if I needed anything. He never thought of helping us. He bought my share of the house with much reluctance."

Efronia informed Ovsannah that she simply would not be married out of her older brother's house. Ovsannah pleaded with her to go for just a few days. Eventually, Efronia agreed. The two women sent their things over with a porter. The few days they spent at Yacoub's felt "like years," Efronia recalls, and finally, one day when Yacoub was out, they announced to his startled wife that they were leaving for Aroussiak's house.

When Yacoub realized what had happened, he rushed home. He was drunk when he arrived. There was a terrible scene. Efronia recalls that she "opened her heart" and finally let her older brother know how she felt about him. She said, "Yacoub, I do not want to leave your house as a bride. But tell me, which single one of your obligations as an older brother, who should have been like a father to us, have you fulfilled? Do you imagine that now, by getting me to leave your house as a bride, you will have fulfilled your responsibilities toward us? I don't want it. I don't accept it. I grew up as an orphan, and I'll be married as an orphan. Let them come and take me from my sister's house. I still love you, and I forgive you, but this wish of yours I will not fulfill."

Yacoub did not utter a sound. He got up and closed the door behind him.

When Efronia left her native Aintab to marry Aram in Aleppo, she left in a most unusual manner. Horse-drawn carriages had long been provincial Turkey's only means of transportation, but because of the war, a few army cars and

191

trucks had appeared in the region, arousing the admiration of the local people.

"There was one car," Efronia used to say with pride. "There was one car available in the entire region. It was a Red Cross ambulance, and Aram managed to rent it from the British Army—for eighteen gold pieces—to take me to my wedding in Aleppo."

The British had finally decided to withdraw from Aintab and French forces were moving in to replace them. Efronia's wedding ambulance left Aintab along with the last retreating convoy of British soldiers, the Indian contingent of General Leslie's Nineteenth Brigade. The retreat left the Armenian community of Aintab extremely worried. Would the French army arrive there soon enough—and would they be strong enough—to fend off the increasing threat of the Turkish nationalist forces?

The political situation cast a pall on the wedding preparations, but for the time being everything was calm. Efronia's party was met outside Aleppo by Aram and eight carriages. The luggage and the trousseau were transferred to these, and an hour later Efronia's party arrived in the large house that Aram had rented for them in Aleppo.

"Aram had rented a nicely furnished house in Aleppo with a long flight of stairs," Efronia writes. "Aram's family had set aside one of the rooms for us to rest in. After we had rested from the journey for a while, they dressed me up in a very beautiful dress that had been made in Aleppo, and we went downstairs. In the dining room, there was a table set with all sorts of dishes, drinks, sweets, and fruits. We ate and drank until late in the evening, when the guests left, and then went to our rooms quite tired. The next day, we spent organizing things and preparing for the wedding. Our wedding was to take place the following day, a Friday evening, in a nice hotel called the Iskenderun."

What did she think when she heard the name of the hotel? Did she wonder why she needed to be reminded, that very day, of the town where she had met Ramzi? She does not say. But is is clear that Efronia went through a magnificent wedding ceremony with a troubled mind. She writes:

The evening of the wedding a woman came over to dress me and do my hair. I wore a splendid wedding dress with a veil that was held in place by a crown. I had a long train made of tulle. The lady also dressed my six beautiful maids of honor; they wore light blue silk dresses and blue ribbons in their hair. They were to walk ahead of me, carrying bouquets. Two other girls were to follow and carry the train.

At six o'clock all the members of the family left for the hotel. The guests were scheduled to arrive at seven. The girls and I stayed behind, along with my brother-in-law, who was going to stand next to me during the wedding ceremony. At seven-thirty, a carriage decorated with ribbons and flowers took us to the hotel. We went up to the hall, which was very large and full of guests. Everyone was very elegantly dressed, with many of the men in tuxedos and the women in long dresses. All were distinguished people.

At one end of the room, two large armchairs had been set out for the bride and groom. On one side was the orchestra of the Nalbandian brothers, with their musicians and singers. Part of the floor was left open for dancing. In another area were two large tables laden with food and sweets, nuts and fruit.

There is a sparseness about Efronia's description of her wedding, as if she has labored over the writing, putting down only the most essential details, making sure we know it was a distinguished affair.

Behind the dutiful description we glimpse Aram, ramrod straight in his waistcoat and fez, his moustache neatly trimmed, his eyes brimming with pride. He was right to be proud: the Nalbandian brothers with their *oud* and drum and violins, their clarinet and *zurna* pipe weaving the happy high notes, were the best band in Aleppo. The room was fragrant with jasmine and roses and carnations, and Aram knew, too, that the wedding feast would be talked about for a long time. He had made sure that the table would be laden with kebabs and stuffed baby lambs, with *sarmas* and *küftes* and marinated sheep's brains, with fish and fruit and sweets. He knew that the *arak* and the wine and the wild cherry liqueur would be flowing and that the dancing, with all the guests locking little fingers to form a chain, would be wild and joyous and go on into the small hours of the morning.

But most of all, he was proud of his chosen bride. He could hardly believe his luck. After all, he was thirty-six. To have had to wait so many years before he could make his offer of marriage to her, to have worried that someone else would marry her before he had his chance—it was a miracle Efronia had remained unmarried this long. He knew she had had many suitors. How lucky he was, he must have said to himself, that no one else had captured her heart!

And there she was now, walking toward him through the crowd, in her pearl-embroidered gown, her beautiful copper-brown hair pulled back into a bun, her large eyes looking straight at him, her large, serious eyes.

When I entered the hall with the maids of honor, the orchestra began to play. Aram came forward and took my arm. The archbishop and his four priests, in their brilliant gowns embroidered with gold thread, were waiting for us on the platform. We stood in front of them, holding hands. Khatchig, the thirteen-year-old son of my brother-in-law Yeghia, was the "godfather" of the wedding and held the cross. It was a glorious wedding.

At the end of the ceremony, Aram and I stood in front of our armchairs. A pearl necklace was placed around my neck. My pearl earrings had already been put on earlier. Everyone came to congratulate us. My brother-in-law Sarkis Effendi passed a pair of gold bracelets onto my wrists. Other close relatives also gave me gold jewelry, so that after a while there was hardly room left to place anything else around my neck or on my arms.

But as the pearl necklace had been put around my neck, I had raised my hand to adjust my veil and noticed that one of my earrings was missing. I was startled. I had a presentiment that something bad was going to happen. My mind was already full of old memories, which kept appearing before my eyes. I kept trying to look happy. But when this happened, it was impossible to be cheerful.

A while later, when we were standing in the reception line, I whispered the news about the earring to Aram. He told me not to worry; he would buy me a better one. But when he saw I was still preoccupied, he sent someone to look for it in the carriage and in the room where I had changed. The earring was nowhere to be found.

When I woke up in the morning, I noticed that the woman who had come to dress me had placed my clothes on the sofa. I was picking them up to hang them in the closet when I heard something fall to the floor. It was my missing earring. It had gotten hooked to my dress. I felt very relieved.

A few months later, she would recall the loss of the earring as an evil omen: Ramzi's memory was to haunt her again.

26

A Shaky Beginning

There is no wedding picture of Efronia and Aram. They had intended to sit for one after the wedding, but this never happened.

In the month after their wedding a steady stream of guests came to the house of the newlyweds to offer their congratulations. Evening after evening, Efronia dressed up in her wedding finery to greet the well-wishers.

Even during the day, the guests never stopped coming. At all times, the couple had to be ready to receive them. Efronia remembers it all as "quite fatiguing." She was struggling to get used to the idea of being married to Aram, to forget her former "dreams."

In November 1920, the couple finally made an appointment to have their wedding picture taken. But just then, they had some alarming news from Aintab. Before the British troops left the town, a French contingent had taken over. The presence of the French was a powerful irritant to the Turks' newfound pride. The war was over, the Turkish reasoning went; there was a new government now, and the Turks and the Armenians should forget the Ottoman past and live in peace with each other. But the Armenians saw the French presence in a different light. They looked to the French as protectors of what remained of their town: a community with few able-bodied men and still fewer arms with which to defend themselves.

It did not take long before the smoldering conflict erupted in pitched battles all over town. In French military lore, the Aintab conflict is referred to as *"le Verdun de l'Anatolie."* The battle raged from house to house, street to street, culminating in four distinct "sieges" that spanned several months and ended with a decisive showdown in November.

The news that had been filtering into Aleppo out of the Armenian section of Aintab was becoming increasingly worrisome. The Armenians were fighting well, but people were starving and supplies were running out. Virtually the whole community was involved: the women and the children carried rocks for the barricades, the men repaired arms and made grenades and gunpowder. In one famous incident, Armenian artisans manufactured a fake cannon that made an enormous noise but could not shoot anything. It was only there to frighten the enemy. In another incident, a French soldier rigged up a row of guns along a rampart where there was a particular shortage of manpower. He then ran from gun to gun, firing them off in rapid succession and creating the illusion of a sizable defending force.

Despite the assurances of the French premier Aristide Briand that the French would not abandon the Armenians, that is exactly what they did. Earlier that year, under similar circumstances, the French had withdrawn from Marash, a provincial town north of Aintab with a sizeable Armenian population. The result was a bloodbath, as the vastly outnumbered Armenians tried to defend themselves. As the French marched away from Aintab, the panicked Armenian community fled with them, except for a handful of families who took refuge in the American missionary hospital compound for three more years.

For Efronia and Aram, who had not yet decided where they would settle, the abandonment of Aintab meant one less alternative. Efronia would never see the town of her birth again, but Aintab would live on in her stories until the end of her life. It was the place where the air was crisp and clear, where sparkling snow covered the ground for three months during the winter, where the fruit was fresh and the nights were cool. In the Armenian diaspora, Efronia was proud to be an *Aintabtsi*.

But the French retreat from Aintab also meant something else for her. It increased the possibility that she would spend the greatest part of her married life in the town where she least of all wanted to be, the town that carried memories she was trying hard to forget.

Even while they were still in Aleppo, Aram's brother Sarkis was telling him about interesting business opportunities in Iskenderun.

Soon after their wedding, Aram and Efronia packed their belongings and took the train from Aleppo for Beirut. The political situation in Aleppo was getting dangerously unstable; Aram wanted to be in a calmer place while he made up his mind about where they would settle permanently.

He spoke with Efronia about this question on a number of occasions. He assured her they would settle in a big city, maybe Smyrna, maybe even Constantinople. Efronia kept urging him to emigrate to America. This was a golden opportunity, she said: the doors to the New World were wide open. Every day, they heard about Armenians who were fast becoming very wealthy there.

But Aram wouldn't listen. "America is too different. You have to work too hard there," he told her. And soon, Smyrna was no longer a possibility—after Mustafa Kemal's forces had ousted the occupying Greeks and turned that fabled city into a flaming inferno. Thousands of Greeks and Armenians lost their lives in that conflagration, in full view of the Allied warships in the harbor, which, in the name of "neutrality," did nothing.

When Aram brought up the subject of going to Iskenderun for a limited time in order to help his brother Sarkis in a business venture, was he surprised by the vehemence of Efronia's objections? Did he ever wonder why she had made him promise, again and again, that they would never settle in Iskenderun? Did he wonder why she became so upset that she would hardly speak to him when he announced, with finality, that they would really have to go there for a limited time? His brother Sarkis could not manage on his own, said Aram, and the business opportunity was too good to pass up.

"I'll go anywhere you like," Efronia told Aram. "Just not Iskenderun. I am telling you right now, if you want to settle in Iskenderun, I'll refuse to go with you."

Efronia pleaded, cried, and threatened, but to no avail. Aram was a stubborn man. Many years later, Efronia could still feel the sting of this conflict, which came close to bringing their marriage to an early end. Of this period, she writes, "We spent several difficult days. Aram could not convince me. The situation became upsetting. I finally realized what a difficult position he was in and decided to trust him when he promised that the move to Iskenderun would be temporary. Later, I regretted this decision a thousand times."

Nevertheless, the decision had been made. Efronia and Aram prepared to go in a few days, and along with the children of Aram's brother Sarkis and a female relative who had accompanied them to Beirut, they boarded a ship for the overnight voyage up the Mediterranean coast and back to Iskenderun.

Years later, Efronia still remembered the pain of that voyage through the hot Mediterranean night, closer and closer to a confrontation with the most painful memories of her life.

As soon as Aram had fallen asleep in their cabin, she left and went up on deck. "The sea was in turmoil, as was my heart," she writes. Sleep was out of the question. As the hours dragged on into morning, she sat in a deck chair, looking out at the sea.

They arrived in Iskenderun in the early morning, just as the sun had climbed high enough in the east to cast some light on the mountains behind the town. It was the hottest time of the year, the same time of year she had first arrived there from Aintab, eight years before.

The ship docked at the Iskenderun pier. Efronia recalls:

The sight of that pier awakened so many unforgettable memories in me. People used to walk on it and watch the sunset over the sea. I could not help remembering the evenings and moonlit nights when Ramzi, Nouriyeh Hanem, and I had strolled there. Things became blurred, and I started to tremble. Aram asked what the matter was, and I told him I was very tired.

I must confess that at that moment I wished I would fall into the sea and that the waves would take me.

Efronia knew that sooner or later she would have to come face to face with Ramzi's ghost. She kept trying to look out for it; she expected, at any moment, to feel its icy hand on her heart.

Meanwhile, there was the charade of the happy bride to play:

Two days after our arrival, we held a reception for people who wished to welcome us and congratulate us on our wedding. We put on our wedding clothes again and welcomed them. A very lavish table was set, with two waiters in attendance. They brought in many delicious dishes, along with cakes, sweets, and all sorts of drinks. The visitors all came with presents and flowers.

Everything was fine except for me. Aram sensed I was indisposed. He approached me many times during the evening and pleaded that I change my mood. He took me to the table so that I would eat something. I knew that my behavior was unforgivable and that I was not going to leave a good impression with the guests. I tried to pull myself together. Seen from the outside, I was an enviable bride. God had created me with perfect beauty, and I had married a presentable young man who was rich and intelligent. I was covered with gold and diamonds. What could I possibly lack?

I knew all this, but I could not help myself. None of it meant anything to me. But I had to reconcile myself to my fate. I had to do my best to pretend I was happy. But in my heart, I wished only that all the guests would leave us as soon as possible so that I could withdraw to my room.

Poor Aram kept circling me, ascribing my mood to my having come to Iskenderun against my will. He could not know what sad and unforgettable memories had been awakened in my heart. Somehow, the evening passed. The guests left, and we went to our room. Aram tried to cheer me up with many sweet words and promises. He begged me to be patient and happy for the next several months, and then we would go and live where we both wanted.

I said nothing. We slept.

All Aram's assurances notwithstanding, Efronia soon realized they had come to Iskenderun to stay. Aram opened a new office overlooking the seashore and furnished it lavishly. He acquired more warehouse space. The business was thriving.

When Efronia pointed out to Aram that these looked to her

like preparations for a permanent stay, Aram turned around, looked at her, and left the room without a word.

"That was when I decided not to bring up the subject anymore," she recalls. "It was no use anyway. I left my fate to God."

Efronia was in no mood to look for redeeming qualities in Iskenderun, but the city had improved while she had been away. People who had fled the war were returning, and there was a lot of rebuilding and renewal, especially of the port, which had been heavily bombed. The French occupying force had drained the swamps, thereby eliminating the mosquitoes that had spread malaria. They had constructed a wide boulevard along the seashore, with coffeehouses and a couple of new clubs. The postwar population was more mixed, more international: in addition to the Turks, there were Armenians, Greeks, Arabs, and some French. The missionary school that Ramzi had attended was still there, run as before by the Scottish Presbyterians from their Damascus headquarters.

The villages up in the mountains overlooking the town were developing into nice summer resorts, with fruit orchards and vineyards thriving in the cool mountain air. This is where Efronia and Aram spent their summers, like so many who would mount mules and horses and trek up there to escape the oppressive summer heat of the coast. Summering in the mountains was a rustic experience in those days of no hotels: the villagers rented their own houses to the townspeople and slept with their animals in the stables. The houses had earthen floors; only a few had kitchen facilities. But the air was crisp and cool, the fruit delicious, the water clear.

In her old age, talking about her relatives, Efronia used to joke: "I don't know why, but wherever Aram and I moved, all our relatives followed. We were like a magnet, attracting them all. I hope that when I die—and that won't be too long now—they don't decide to follow me to heaven, everyone all at once."

She had a point. There was always a big crowd of relatives following them: from Aintab to Aleppo, from Aleppo to Iskenderun; later, from Iskenderun to Beirut; and much later still, from Beirut to the United States. The magnet, for many of them, was Aram. His business acumen made him ever more wealthy. He was also generous. Gradually, he took on the financial responsibility for a wide network of needy relatives. He fed and housed widows and orphans, he put young men through school, he helped start others in business, he supported those who were simply not willing to work as hard as he was. To Iskenderun they all came, and with Aram's help, they all put down roots in the town.

Efronia soon realized that to get Aram to leave Iskenderun, even a few months after they had arrived, would have meant severe hardship for many of their relatives.

She would just have to try to live with Ramzi's ghost. But that was going to be even more difficult than she had imagined.

This was driven home to Efronia when a friend came to her with a startling piece of news.

27

Ramzi's Ghost

All during those first months of settling in and getting to know people of Iskenderun in her new role as a married woman, Efronia had been hoping against hope that none of Ramzi's relatives would ever return. She knew that Nouriyeh Hanem had spent the war years in Ankara and that Ramzi's parents had left the town, too. But all along, she had a premonition that her past with Ramzi would catch up with her, and she was not altogether surprised when a friend came and said she had some news for her.

"You'll be very happy to hear this, Efronia," said the friend. "Your old friend Nouriyeh Hanem is moving back here with her family. We're inviting all her friends for dinner, and we'd love to have you and Aram come, too."

Efronia's heart sank. She tried as best she could to look pleased, and promised to talk to her husband. There was no getting away from this, she thought. She would be forced to socialize with the woman who had introduced her to Ramzi. This was her reward for consenting to move to Iskenderun.

She relayed the invitation to Aram, hoping he would be in an unsociable mood. But no, Aram had never met Nouriyeh Hanem, he said, although he did have some business dealings with her husband, Shakib Bey, whom he liked and respected. He saw no reason why they should not go to the dinner.

When Efronia and Nouriyeh Hanem met that night, they

caused a lot of consternation by falling into each other's arms and sobbing. Someone reminded them that people generally laugh when they are reunited, and Nouriyeh Hanem, through her tears, tried to explain that they simply were weeping with joy. The explanation was accepted. After all, what other reason could there possibly have been for this show of emotion?

Nouriyeh Hanem now began to come for frequent visits. Efronia details the renewed friendship in these words:

Neither of us mentioned the past at first; we were most careful. In a few weeks, she invited all of us to the club for dinner, since she and Shakib Bey had not yet furnished their house.

I now had three close friends: Nouriyeh Hanem and two other ladies. I am glad there were virtually no narrow-minded Armenians in our circle in Iskenderun. It was a small town, and some there envied me and gossiped about my past. We paid no attention to them.

Life went on uneventfully. My social life gave me great pleasure. But I very much regret that this pleasant state of affairs lasted only for a few months. There is a proverb that says, "Boiling water does not stay in the pot; sooner or later, it boils over." That is exactly what happened to me.

Sooner or later, the subject of Ramzi was bound to come up.

One day, Nouriyeh Hanem and I started talking about the past. She turned to me and said, "My dear friend, forgive me, but in the past you took some bad steps. Your family should have accepted Ramzi's proposal—especially at that time when the Armenians were being persecuted by the Turks, when they were being murdered, deported to the desert, and tortured, and when their young and attractive girls were being abducted and dishonored.

"Ramzi's father knew that his son loved you with all his heart and that he wanted to marry you. He wrote to Ramzi innumerable times and told him to bring you to London and save you from danger. 'I am certain,' he said, 'that terrible things are going to happen to

the Armenians. My son, write to Efronia and say that your father wants her to go to school until you yourself finish your education and that all her expenses will be borne by me.' "

Nouriyeh Hanem went on for almost an hour. Beginning to cry, I said to her, "Do you think my whole family knew about my relationship with Ramzi? Only my mother and my oldest sister knew. And my mother opposed us; only my sister was in favor of our getting married. I was certain my brothers would have scolded me and blamed me and created difficulties for me. I had to carry this cross to Golgotha by myself. Everybody was going to dwell on the fact that I was an Armenian and Ramzi was a Moslem; no one knew that Ramzi was prepared to bear every sacrifice, even to change his religion and become baptized in our church for my sake. My dear friend, for four years I lived as a prisoner in our house, with my heart on fire. We were saved by a miracle. Otherwise, we would have been exiled to Deir Zor, and our entire family would have been lost."

I told Nouriyeh Hanem about Ramzi's visit to Aintab, about those happy and desperate fifteen days we had passed together in the shadow of the war, about how I had felt certain I would never see him again after he left me in Beshgüz.

When I had finished, Nouriyeh Hanem was very moved and only said quietly: "It was a great pity. He did not deserve to die so young. He suffered much. Münever Hanem must have told you the circumstances of his death."

"Yes," I said weakly. "They told me about the car accident. They told me his parents had gone to London."

"Did you also hear," asked Nouriyeh Hanem, "that after he died and they took his bed covers and his clothes off, they found a photograph of you on his chest?"

On hearing this, I almost lost myself.

Nouriyeh Hanem must have realized she had gone too far. She suggested they try to put Ramzi behind them. He was gone, and all his dreams with him. There was no use dwelling on the past. Efronia told herself the same thing. It was not fair to Aram; she would have to get on with her life.

"That day," she writes, "I made myself a promise in front of God. I told my dear Ramzi, that even though death had separated us, I would never forget him. His memory would remain in my heart until the day I died. Yet at the same time, I would be a good wife to my husband, who loved me so much, and not cause him unhappiness because of my memories. From that day on, I lived up to my promise."

It was a simple compromise: Efronia could hold onto her memories of Ramzi, just as long as she was a dutiful wife to Aram. Thinking about Ramzi was acceptable. Getting upset by those thoughts was not.

Soon enough, her resolve would be severely tested.

"I want to ask you a great favor, Efronia," said Nouriyeh Hanem one day. "I know it will be hard for you, but I hope you won't refuse."

"Please, what is it?"

"You know that Ramzi's family was in Persia during the war. Efronia, they are back in town now. Ramzi's mother knows you are here and that you are married. Farouz Hanem is longing to see you. But she has not been able to bring herself to visit you. She is concerned that someone might see your reunion, see the two of you crying, and wonder why.

"Efronia, she begs me to bring you to her house. She pleaded so much that I couldn't say no. I told her I would ask you."

Efronia remained silent for a long time. She dreaded the prospect of seeing Ramzi's mother, but she simply could not bring herself to say no. At worst, she told herself, they would both get very upset. Efronia knew that Farouz Hanem wished to see her because she was a link to the older woman's beloved son. What right, she asked herself, did she have to deprive Farouz Hanem of this?

Late one afternoon, as the sun was beginning to set, Efronia and Nouriyeh Hanem knocked on Ramzi's mother's door.

She was still living in the same house where she had lived in 1913. The loquat trees in the garden had grown, but otherwise nothing much had changed. Farouz Hanem opened the door; as soon as she and Efronia saw each other, they fell into each other's arms and broke into tears.

Then Farouz Hanem told Efronia that she wanted to show her the house. She took her by the hand, and slowly they began to walk through the rooms.

We came to a room right opposite the living room. The door was locked. Farouz Hanem took out a key and opened the door, and we entered.

The first thing I saw, right there on the wall, was an enormous enlargement of a photograph of me and Ramzi, the last picture ever taken of us. We were holding each other's hands.

An embroidered cap had been attached to Ramzi's head on the photograph. And to my head there was fastened a beautiful veil covered with flowers.

I was speechless.

I stared at the photograph for a long time, and then I turned around. I saw Ramzi's bed. His silk pajamas lay on it, as if waiting for him to change into them, and his robe was hanging over the side.

I had no idea what happened next. Everything went black. I must have fainted.

The shock of this encounter sent Efronia to bed for a month. Farouz Hanem visited her a few times and brought her flowers. They saw each other occasionally after that, and eventually the family moved back to Persia. Then Nouriyeh Hanem moved to Antioch; she visited once in a while, but never again was the past brought up.

Efronia and Aram remained in Iskenderun until 1939. Aram's business flourished. He owned land and houses and was a trusted and prominent member of Iskenderun society. Efronia was one of its glittering ladies—her dresses came from Le Printemps in Paris, her grand piano from Berlin, her jewelry from the finest jeweler in Constantinople. A retinue of servants took care of practical matters, and Efronia kept busy with an active social life, piano lessons, and volunteer work.

But as Efronia moved about in Iskenderun society, she was keenly aware that there were many tongues wagging about her. Look, they said, here is this woman who has everything, but what good does it do her? She has not been able to fulfill her duty as a wife and produce an heir.

When Efronia failed to conceive during the first few years of her marriage, she initially was not concerned. There were other children in her life. Yacoub, who lived nearby, had two daughters and a son. He had become a respected member of the community and reconciled with his sister. Yacoub's second daughter, Elvira, was a frequent visitor at Efronia's house. When she was barely four, Elvira declared that she was going to be Aunt Efronia's daughter. And that, in effect, is what she became, though Efronia and Aram never formally adopted her. Years later, Efronia would also help bring up Yervant's daughter, Nora, after her parents separated.

Then there was Lucine. She was one of thousands of Armenian children who had lost their families in the genocide. Lucine, mercifully, had no memory of her parents nor any idea of what had happened to them. She had been placed in an orphanage in Beirut run by Danish missionaries, and from there, at age fourteen, she came to the Katchadourians in Iskenderun. She clung to Efronia for dear life.

These ties partly fulfilled Efronia's deep yearning for a child, yet she still desperately wanted to bear her own.

She had tried everything from doctors to folk cures. She had a midwife come and "massage the uterus into place." She avoided drinking very cold water so the uterus wouldn't contract and make conception difficult; she accepted Grandmother Trvandah's blue beads and sewed them into her underwear to avert bad luck; she went on a pilgrimage to Jerusalem. Above all, she hoped and prayed.

Gradually, she came to feel as if her silent, secret longing for Ramzi and her wish for a child were merging into one, aching inside her, trying to fill the same emptiness.

After ten years and several miscarriages, Aram and Efronia decided to go to Beirut to consult a specialist. The news was encouraging.

"There is nothing wrong," the doctor told them. "Go home, and be patient. One day soon, I'm certain you'll have a baby."

And, indeed, Efronia became pregnant soon after they returned from Beirut. It was a difficult pregnancy. She had severe morning sickness, and in the seventh month she started spotting. She was sick with worry. Was she about to have another miscarriage? She was turning forty that year; this might be her last chance.

Efronia spent the rest of her pregnancy in bed.

Late one evening in January 1933, the news that Efronia had gone into labor traveled like a hot wind from the desert among the relatives in Iskenderun. Everybody gathered at the Katchadourians' house. The first night passed with no news. Messengers kept running back and forth between the house and the hospital. Aram kept pacing the corridors. Efronia's labor continued on through the day and all through another night. On the evening of the third day, a cloud of worry had settled over the family.

No one said much. An old aunt was mumbling her prayers. But just as Lucine brought a silver tray with sixteen cups of Turkish coffee into the living room, they heard the sound of a bicycle being flung to the ground at the door of the house. Someone was shouting something, and then Efronia's nephew Puzant burst through the door.

"A boy!" he shouted. "It's a boy!"

Lucine dropped the tray and all sixteen cups of coffee on the Tabriz rug in the living room. It was considered an excellent omen.

They called the baby Herant. He became the center of Efronia's life, and Lucine became his nanny.

In 1939, just before the Second World War, the area around Iskenderun, which had been a semi-autonomous part of the French Syrian mandate, was ceded to Turkey to satisfy its insistent claims. A plebiscite had been held that was rigged in favor of Turkey. The French accepted the outcome, since with the threat of war on the horizon, they were in no position to alienate the Turks. This made the Armenians who were living in the city very nervous. They could not see going through another war as Turkish subjects, and soon enough, almost all the Armenians in the region of Iskenderun accepted the French offer to resettle them in Syria or Lebanon.

Efronia urged Aram to liquidate his holdings and get out. But Aram could not contemplate abandoning the fruits of so many years of successful labor. The Katchadourians stayed behind for another year, but as World War II heated up, they left for Beirut, with just a couple of suitcases, for what they thought would be a short visit. Once they were there, however, their relatives and friends prevailed on them not to return to Iskenderun.

Aram dealt with the loss of his fortune by hardly ever talking about it. Efronia, too, was philosophical. But their sudden departure meant another loss for her that we learned about only after reading her memoir.

Efronia told us that a few days before she and Aram were to leave their Iskenderun house, she had asked the gardener to dig a hole near a big tree in the back garden. In this hiding place, she hurriedly buried all her tangible memories of Ramzi: his letters to her, the locket with their pictures, her secret engagement ring.

In a month or so, she had told herself, I'll come back and dig them up again.

28

Medzmama

One day, soon after Herant and I had returned to Beirut from our wedding in Finland, Efronia took me aside.

"Look, *aghchigs*," she said, "my daughter, I know what it was like to have only one child. It is not good; a girl needs a sister to play with. A boy needs a brother. I tell you, have at least four. A big family is very nice."

At that point, I wasn't even pregnant yet.

Efronia would have to wait a few years to become a *medzmama*. The news of her granddaughter Nina's birth came over the telephone from California. It caused great joy among the Beirut relatives; many telegrams arrived, and much gold jewelry. But that was nothing compared to the riotous outburst of jubilation at the news of the birth of our second child, Kai Aram. This one was a boy.

At first, Efronia had to play her grandmotherly role from a distance, but she didn't let it deter her. Long before our daughter's birth, packages from Beirut started arriving: swaddling cloths, masterfully knit small sweaters and dresses from Lucine with small beads sewn into the seams to ward off the evil eye. Later came enormous stuffed animals, a rabbit-fur coat, all manner of battery-driven creatures that danced and did somersaults and made music. And loving letters that always ended with "I kiss your beautiful eyes, Your loving *Medzmama*."

Efronia was bonded to her grandchildren with strong bio-logical ties that eliminated barriers of language and culture. As *Medzmama* in California, she was content if she could just see them, or even smell them. No amount of time spent with them seemed too long. Nothing was good enough for them, and there was no amount of misbehaving or messing up that could not be excused by the fact that they were still "very young."

To her, everything the grandchildren did was simply the best. No one sat more erect or applauded longer at school drama performances or piano recitals than *Medzmama* and Lucine. No one cheered more loudly at the sidelines of Saturday morning soccer games. No one could last longer through a loud drum solo, or admire a Halloween costume more, or display a stick-figure drawing in a more prominent place.

She thought being asked to baby-sit was simply the best thing that could happen to her. When we left the house and the two children with *Medzmama* and Lucine, we knew our home was about to be taken over by a Gang of Four. Favorite and forbidden food would be smuggled in, football games—with Efronia as quarterback—would break out in the living room, houses would be constructed of furniture, pillows, and blankets. And after these games, what else could Efronia do for her poor darlings but let them sit and rest in front of the television for as long as they wanted, restore their energy by bringing them food, and finally excuse them from cleaning up on the grounds that the games had been "too tiring."

At the end of all this, groggy with sleep and full of chocolate and ice cream, they would be escorted to their bedrooms, simply "too sleepy" to brush their teeth.

When we got home, we would invariably find *Medzmama* outside one of the children's bedrooms and Lucine outside the other, both of them knitting in the semi-darkness of the corridor, "just so the children won't be afraid." And like magic, all the laundry in the house would have been done and ironed and folded, and every loose button sewed back on, and every torn pair of jeans patched, and every last dish washed and in its place in the cupboard.

This extravagant love only grew as the years went by. Even as Efronia's consciousness was fading away during her final illness, the mere mention of one of her grandchildren would bring her back, alert and awake.

During her final month, she was mostly dozing, slipping away. A letter arrived from her granddaughter in college.

"*Medzmama*," I whispered, "there is a letter from Nina. She sends you her love."

In an instant, Efronia's eyes opened, her lips trying to form words. "*Sireli tornigs*. My dear grandchild. May God protect her."

"*Medzmama*, Kai got his driver's license today."

"God bless him. When I get well, I will go for a ride with him."

Efronia was magnificent until the very last. When reality no longer was within her grasp, she made up her own. She ordered packages of food to be sent to faraway relatives, some of them long dead. She demanded an umbrella to protect her from the rain and warm boots with which to walk through the snows of Aintab. She asked Lucine to keep the brazier of her childhood living room burning and sent her out to pick olives and peppers to put by for the winter.

Images of the dead swirled through her memory: her mother and her two sisters, long gone; Yervant's lingering death from cirrhosis; Yacoub's despair and suicide when he was an old man.

Her son spent long hours sitting by her bedside in her home, massaging her back and arms, holding her hand. Did she know who was sitting there? Once, when I caught her looking at Herant, I could see that the man she had once loved and the son she brought up to be like him had finally in her eyes merged into one.

One day shortly before the end, Efronia stirred in her bed, opened her eyes wide, and began to say something. Her speech had a beautiful, rhythmic quality to it, and it seemed to emerge from a great inner calm. I recognized the language. It was Turkish. But I couldn't understand the words.

"It's the Lord's Prayer," whispered Lucine.

Efronia was looking far into the distance. Her voice was steady:

Forgive our trespasses.
As we forgive those who trespass against us.

Bibliography

Abajian, Heghine, in collaboration with Gil Haroian. *On a Darkling Plain*. Fairlawn, N.J.: Rosekeer Press, 1984.

Baronian, Haig. *Barefoot Boy from Anatolia*. Los Angeles: Abril Printing Co., 1983.

Bedrossyan, Mark D. *The First Genocide of the 20th Century*. Flushing, N.Y.: Voskedar Publishing, 1983.

Beliozian, Ara. *The Armenians: Their History and Culture*. Saddle Brook, N.J.: AGBU Ararat Press, 1980.

Boase, T. S. R., ed. *The Cilician Kingdom of Armenia*. Edinburgh: Scottish Academic Press, 1978.

Boyajian, Dickran H. *Armenia, The Case for a Forgotten Genocide*. Westwood, N.J.: Educational Book Crafters, 1972.

Davidson, Khoren K. *Odyssey of an Armenian of Zeitoun*. New York: Vantage Press, 1985.

Dobkin, Marjorie Housepian. *Smyrna 1922: Destruction of a City*. Kent, Ohio: Kent State University Press, 1988.

Grabill, Joseph L. *Protestant Diplomacy and the Near East, 1810–1927*. Minneapolis: University of Minnesota Press, 1971.

Hartunian, Abraham H. *Neither to Laugh Nor to Weep*. Trans. Vartan Hartunian. 2d ed. Cambridge, Mass.: Armenian Heritage Press, 1986.

Highas, Dirouhi Kouymijian. *Refugee Girl*. Watertown, Mass.: Baikar Publications, 1985.

Hovannisian, Richard. *The Armenian Holocaust, A Bibliography Relating to the Deportations, Massacres, and Dispersion of the Armenian People, 1915–1923*. Cambridge, Mass.: Armenian Heritage Press, 1978.

Hovannisian, Richard. *Armenia on the Road to Independence*. Berkeley: University of California Press, 1967.

Hovannisian, Richard, ed. *The Armenian Genocide in Perspective*. New Brunswick, N.J.: Transaction Books, 1986.

Kerr, Stanley E. *The Lions of Marash*. Albany: State University of New York Press, 1973.

Kherdian, David. *The Road from Home: The Story of an Armenian Girl*. New York: Greenwillow Books, 1979.

Long, David Marshall, and Christopher J. Walker. *The Armenians*. Minority Rights Group International, London, Report No. 32, February 1987.

Lynch, H. F. B. *Armenia, Travels and Studies*. 2 vols. London, 1901; repr. Beirut: Khayats, 1965.

Melson, Robert F. *Revolution and Genocide*. Chicago: University of Chicago Press, 1992.

Morgenthau, Henry. *Ambassador Morgenthau's Story*. New York: Doubleday, 1919; repr. New York: New Age Publishers, 1975.

Nalbandian, Louise. *The Armenian Revolutionary Movement*. Berkeley: University of California Press, 1967.

Pears, Sir Edwin. *Life of Abdul Hamid*. London: Constable & Co., 1917.

Permanent Peoples' Tribunal. *A Crime of Silence: The Armenian Genocide*. Trans. Gerard Chaliand. London: Zed Books, 1985.

Richter, Julius. *A History of Protestant Missions in the Near East*. 1910; repr. New York: AMS Press, 1970.

Ternon, Yves. *The Armenians: History of a Genocide*. Trans. Rouben C. Cholakian. New York: Caravan Books, 1981.

Topalian, Naomi. *Dust to Destiny*. Watertown, Mass.: Baikar Publications, 1986.

Toynbee, Arnold J. *Armenian Atrocities: The Murder of a Nation*. Preface by Lord Bryce. London: Hodder and Stoughton, 1915.

Villa, Susie Hoogasian, and Mary Kilbourne Matossian. *Armenian Village Life Before 1914*. Detroit: Wayne State University Press, 1982.

Walker, Christopher J. *Armenia*. Rev. 2d ed. New York: St. Martin's, 1990.

Werfel, Franz. *The Forty Days of Musa Dagh*. New York: Viking Press, 1935.

Zaroukian, Andranik. *Men without Childhood*. Trans. Elise Bayizian and Marzbed Margossian. New York: Ashod Press, 1985.